Partnering With Parents

Acknowledgments

Special thanks to the many students in the Family Involvement classes at Southern Illinois University, Edwardsville, who over the past 34 years have provided many ideas for a number of the meetings in this book. In particular, thanks to the following students in CI 421, Child, Family, and Community Relationships (Spring 2002): Jeremy Heigert, Rebecca Jack, Julie Kelly, Jenni Nelson, Stacey Qualls, Shelly Richards, Melinda Schulmeister, Vicki Steibel, Courtney Ulm, and Heather Wilde. Thanks also to Isabel Baker, President of the Book Vine for Children (and the BEST story reader ever!) for providing the literacy listings for each family meeting. And last, but hardly the least, our editor ~ Kathy Charner, for her understanding and encouragement, as well as her professional expertise during the book's production.

Dedication

Thanks to my mother and father (co-author!) for their never-ending encouragement and support so dreams can come true.

To Katie, Michael, and Wayne with all my love. Thanks for your patience and understanding.

—Janet Rockwell Kniepkamp

To my wife, Donna, our daughters, Janet (co-author) and Susan, my grandchildren, Teri, Robert, Amanda, Katie, and Michael for the lessons they have taught me, the love they have given, and the joy they have provided.

—Bob Rockwell

Partnering With Parents

Easy Programs to Involve Parents in the Early Learning Process

Robert E. Rockwell and Janet Rockwell Kniepkamp

Illustrations by K. Whelan Dery

gryphon house
Beltsville, MD

Published by Gryphon House, Inc.
10726 Tucker Street, Beltsville, MD 20705
or P.O. Box 207, Beltsville, MD 20704-0207.
(800) 638-0928, (301) 595-9500, (301) 595-0051 (Fax)

Visit us on the web at www.gryphonhouse.com

Illustrations: K. Whelan Dery

Library of Congress Cataloging-in-Publication Data

Rockwell, Robert E.
   Partnering with parents : easy programs to involve parents in the early learning process / by Robert E. Rockwell and Janet Rockwell Kniepkamp ; illustrations, K. Whelan Dery.
      p. cm.
Includes index.
   ISBN: 978-0-87659-231-1
   1. Early childhood education--Parent participation. 2. Parent-teacher relationships. 3. Home and school. I. Kniepkamp, Janet Rockwell. II. Title.
   LB1139.35.P37R62 2003
   372.119'2--dc21

                                               2002155787

Gryphon House is a member of the Green Press Initiative, a nonprofit program dedicated to supporting publishers in their efforts to reduce their use of fiber-sourced forests. This book is made of 30% post-consumer waste. For further information visit www.greenpressinitiative.org.

Bulk purchase
Gryphon House books are available at special discount when purchased in bulk for special premiums and sales promotions as well as for fund-raising use. Special editions or book excerpts also can be created to specification. For details, contact the Director of Marketing at Gryphon House.

Disclaimer
Gryphon House, Inc. and the authors cannot be held responsible for damage, mishap, or injury incurred during the use of or because of activities in this book. Appropriate and reasonable caution and adult supervision of children involved in activities and corresponding to the age and capability of each child involved, is recommended at all times. Do not leave children unattended at any time. Observe safety and caution at all times. Every effort has been made to locate copyright and permission information.

Table of Contents

Are You Hungry for Family Fun?
To demonstrate how children's literature can be integrated into daily curricular activities.

Bananas About Books
To create a sense of partnership while developing materials that can be used at home to foster literacy experiences for children.

Bright Ideas
To encourage families to recognize problems and learn to work through them together.

Castles to Moats and Shovels to Boats
To develop gross and fine motor skills, to explore creative uses of sand and water, and to interact with others cooperatively.

Family Bookworms

To promote literacy awareness and provide families with literature and literacy activities to promote a lifelong interest in reading.

Family Game Night

To explore games as means of enhancing children's social, cognitive, and motor skills.

Get Ready, Get Set, Move!

To develop physical skills, including competency in body management and spatial movement, and manipulative skills, while participating in a non-competitive, non-threatening manner.

The Great Graphing Safari

To present a range of activities that offer opportunities to collect, share, and compare information using graphs, and to reinforce counting, letter recognition, and fine motor skills.

INTRODUCTION

What Is Family Involvement?

Many programs have defined parent involvement through a model that uses a specific format for parent-educator interventions, such as home visitation, conferences, or parent education classes. Yet, parent involvement exists in a broad continuum of activities and strategies. Parent involvement, therefore, is any activity that empowers parents and families to participate in the educational process, either at home or in a program setting. Every family involvement program is based on a philosophy of child-adult and adult-adult interaction that assigns roles to both parent and educator. This book focuses on one strategy: The family meeting. Educating children has become a shared responsibility among families, childcare programs, and schools. Early childhood educators recognize the need for communication and collaboration with parents and families of children. The family meeting format has proven to be an excellent strategy for establishing a reciprocal relationship between home and school. This relationship, once established, enhances a program's positive impact on child development and develops and strengthens home-school connections.

Family meetings can establish a bridge (connection) from the home to the school or the center that allows families to have a valued and meaningful presence in the program. Family members' time, skills, and experience are shared at the meetings. Establishing a sense of community and developing new friendships with other families also occurs. This home-school bridge also allows staff members to bring pertinent, curricular information to the families.

Although family meetings are the focus of this book, it is evident that the concept of family involvement encompasses a variety of options. Commitment is key to them all. Without the dedication and perseverance of early childhood administrators, educators, and the families they serve, early education would lose one of the most valuable factors in effective programming: family involvement.

The Value of Family Involvement

Getting together with families in group meetings offers teachers an excellent strategy to promote family involvement. The family meetings in this book provide a supportive and friendly environment in which learning activities can be presented optimally. After getting acquainted in an informal setting, families can overcome initial social anxiety and become actively involved in activities. There are many advantages to families and teachers working together in group meetings, including:

- Families develop new friendships.
- Families learn from other families.
- Individual parents and guardians become involved.
- Families gain new insight and understanding about the curriculum.
- Families develop an awareness of developmentally appropriate teaching and learning practices and how they are helpful both at school and at home.
- Families gain appreciation for teacher's efforts.
- Parents are better able to define appropriate levels of expectations for their child's development and begin to perceive their child's developing abilities and skills.
- Parents feel more comfortable in their interactions with teachers.
- Parents develop an appreciation of their own abilities.

It is critical that early childhood educators reach parents early, as the process that contributes to school success begins when a child is born. "Many children drop out before they drop in. The seeds of failure are sown early, and early intervention is critical" (Jones, 1989).

Research with school-aged children over the past 40 years finds that family involvement is critical to the educational success of both the child and the school, in part, because it:

- Raises the academic achievement of students
- Improves the attitudes and performances of children in school
- Has a positive effect on self-esteem and motivation to learn
- Reduces behavior problems and lowers dropout rates
- Helps parents understand and be more supportive of school or center curriculum content, policies, and procedures
- Builds school-community relationships in an ongoing, problem-preventing way
- Gives teachers an opportunity to get acquainted with the family and learn about their concerns, which, in turn, helps them respond to their needs

Children who attend school meetings with their parents are often sent to a separate room where childcare is provided. This is appropriate if the topic of the meeting is an adult issue or concern. However, we feel that having the entire family together actively participating in a variety of curricular activities will help them leave the meeting with a better understanding of what the program is trying to do and how they can extend this approach to learning with their children at home. Teachers, in turn, also learn and understand more about the families. A meeting should never pass without the reminder of how critical it is for parents and teachers to work together as partners in the education of the children.

There are many types of family meetings, including roundtable discussions, brainstorming, role playing, lectures, and informal workshops. (See Rockwell, Andre, and Hawley, Harcourt Brace (1996) for a discussion of types of family meetings.) No single approach will meet all group needs, so teachers and families must work together to match meeting formats to stated needs, strengths, personal characteristics, and school cultures. Although all the meetings in this book are planned for attendance by the entire family, there will be a need for some meetings that are inappropriate for children to attend. In that case, be sure that adequate childcare is available to enable all family members to attend.

The authors have tried all of the formats with varying degrees of success. Over the years we have found that families have overwhelmingly favored family meetings with an informal workshop/station format because it allows them to be actively involved with a hands-on approach as they interact with their children.

What Is a Family Meeting?

All of the meetings presented in this book use the same organizational format, which includes all the information a teacher needs to present a successful meeting. Each family meeting in this book includes the following components:

Content Area(s): Curricular area(s) that the meeting addresses.
Title: A suggested title for the meeting that is catchy and upbeat and certain to get the attention of the families.
Purpose: The reason for the meeting and what it will try to accomplish.
Invitation: Information sent to the home at least two weeks in advance to announce the meeting. Provides title, content, date, time (including when the family meeting will end), and location. Also gives

suggestion for type of dress and contact name for additional information and to make a reservation for the family meeting. (Permission to photocopy invitation granted.)

Reminder: A friendly hint to help parents remember the forthcoming workshop, sent home one to three days before the meeting. (Permission to photocopy reminder granted.)

Nametag: Used to identify participants and to facilitate station rotation.

Mixer: An activity designed to make the participants feel welcome, get acquainted with each other, and set a fun, relaxing tone for the meeting. It also corresponds to the meeting content.

Introduction: Helpful information relating to meeting content and procedures that will be followed regarding initial station assignment and rotation procedure.

Stations: Areas that are set up where families participate in hands-on activities, following a time schedule. A signal (bell, whistle, and so on) is given when it is time to move to the next station. There are three to five stations for each meeting. Each station is titled, has a list of materials needed, advance preparation information if needed, and step-by-step procedures to be followed by participants.

Evaluation: Forms that require a simple mark (circling or underlining a character) and also provide space for comments, should participants wish to write reactions. The design of the evaluation forms is sensitive to individuals with limited English language proficiency. (Permission to photocopy evaluation forms granted.)

Literacy Connections: Each meeting provides a suggested list of children's books that embellish and expand on meeting content. These books will be helpful for both families and teachers.

Refreshments: We recommend that refreshments be provided at meetings. They need not be expensive or elaborate. Cookies or pretzels and coffee or juice contribute to a relaxed atmosphere that is conducive to families and teachers sharing and working together as partners.

How This Book Is Organized

This book contains a sequence of family meetings that are designed to involve the entire family (children and adults) in hands-on curricular activities utilizing a workshop format. Curricular areas addressed are: art, music and movement, literacy, language, science, motor skills, math, dramatic play, sand and water play, social studies (learning about the community), social development, science, problem solving and critical thinking, nutrition, outdoors, and multicultural diversity.

Strategies for Successful Family Meetings

Some educators are reluctant to use family meetings because they are afraid families will not attend the meetings. Over a 30-year period, the authors have interviewed parents in 35 states about obstacles to attending family meetings. The following are obstacles to attendance and possible solutions:

Obstacles	Solutions
Families receive late notification.	Send home an invitation to the meeting at least two weeks in advance. Send home one or more reminder notes the week of the meeting.
Meetings are not held at convenient times.	Schedule meetings in different time slots. Try a variety of meeting times: morning, before school, during school, after school, and weekends. Do this in consideration of families who have work schedules that prohibit them from attending afternoon and evening meetings.
No childcare is provided.	Although this book focuses on meetings for the entire family, there will be times when a meeting's agenda will have an adult-only focus. For these meetings, provide childcare by competent caregivers in a safe environment. Care providers should be more than just a few years older than the children. The room where care is provided should be well equipped with cribs and toys that are appropriate for a wide range of ages.
Parents are not included in planning topics of interest to them.	Give parents numerous opportunities for input on meeting topics of interest to them. Ask for this input after the parents are acquainted with each other and staff members. Usually by the second or third meeting, trust has been established and parents feel their input matters.
Meetings do not start or finish on time.	It is critical that all meetings begin and end as scheduled. It is irritating to arrive at a meeting on time and then be forced to wait 15 to 20 minutes for latecomers. Both families and staff appreciate starting and ending a meeting as scheduled.
Meetings are too long.	A good length of time is 1 to 1½ hours.
Teachers complain when family attendance is small.	While it is normal to feel disappointed when only a few families show up for a meeting, present the meeting as planned with the same enthusiasm you would have if all the families had attended. Word will spread about the great meeting that so many missed, and the next meeting should show an increase in attendance. This may take more than one meeting to achieve as parents may recall past unproductive meetings.
Meetings are too formal.	Informal or casual is the most popular dress for meetings. It is important to let parents know about how to dress, using the meeting invitation and the reminder notice.

15

No refreshments are served.	Refreshments are a critical component of a meeting. They do not have to be expensive or elaborate. Cookies or crackers and coffee or juice can contribute to a relaxed atmosphere.
No transportation is provided.	Some programs have found that families have no way to get to the meeting. This is a problem that should not be ignored. Some programs offer bus service, while others offer rides with other families and teachers who have cars.
A small clique of parents dominates meetings.	This is a problem that cannot be tolerated. Be assertive! Make certain that all present feel comfortable to participate.
Parents are not given an opportunity to evaluate meetings.	Parents and teachers should evaluate all meetings. The results should be used to plan future meeting topics of interest to families. Invite parents to choose or suggest topics for future meetings.

Guidelines for Planning Family Meetings

Develop a Purpose: All meetings need a purpose. Before planning a meeting, ask yourself what you want to accomplish with this meeting. Whether the purpose is to introduce families to the program curriculum, to get acquainted with each other, or to recruit volunteers, do not proceed without sharing this information with the families.

Choose a Topic and Title: The title of the meeting is important. It should be something catchy and upbeat. For example, the title "Healthful Snacks" can be upgraded to "Raisin' Your Nutritional I.Q." The title "Dealing with Stress" might be more appealing as "How to Make Stress Work for You."

Deliver Advance Information to Families: Inform families about the meeting well ahead of time. This can be accomplished by sending an invitation to the home. The invitation should describe the meeting and include such information as who, what, where, when, why, dress (informal or formal), and whether childcare is available and whether refreshments will be served. It should also include a number to call or an email address to RSVP or obtain further information. Send the invitation at least two weeks before the meeting. Send it home again one to three days before the event as a reminder.

Develop a Planning Schedule: A schedule is essential for planning and conducting the meeting. Schedules can solve problems in advance and eliminate chaos and wasted time. An example of a planning schedule for a family meeting follows.

INTRODUCTION

One month before the meeting:
1. Decide on a topic that fits program and family needs.
2. Clear and set a date and time.
3. Reserve a room or outdoor space.
4. Contact the personnel involved (co-workers, volunteers, speakers and so on).

Two weeks before the meeting:
1. Send out invitations.
2. Arrange for transportation and childcare if needed.
3. List supplies needed and begin to collect them.
4. Reaffirm the date, time, and place.

One week before the meeting:
1. Duplicate handout materials.
2. Make nametags.
3. Organize supplies.

Three days before the meeting:
1. Send out reminders.

One day before the meeting:
1. Make reminder calls or send emails.
2. Check with custodian to arrange for extra chairs, tables, key, and so on.
3. Buy refreshments.

Day of the meeting:
1. Ask the children to remind their families about the meeting.
2. Arrange the room; set up each station.
3. Make sure you have all the necessary materials.
4. Prepare the refreshments.
5. Arrive early!

Tips for Dividing into Groups

When using stations, it is important to keep the number of people at each station as equal as possible. Additionally, family members should all be at the same station so they can spend their time together at the meeting. With a bit of pre-planning, this process will go smoothly.

Begin by having an equal number of nametags for each station. Be sure to have extra nametags on hand in case families show up without a reservation or notification that they were coming. Since families are encouraged to return their reservations prior to each meeting, tentatively divide the participants by writing their names on a piece of paper that has a list of the meeting's stations. Use that list when the families register at the meeting so family members receive the correct nametags and mark names off the list after the families arrive. Also, make tally marks showing an actual count of the people at each station. Some pre-registered families may not be able to attend the meeting, or you may have some families attend that did not return their reservation slip. If so, then adjust the groups at registration for the meeting. Tally marks are helpful to see how many people are at each station, and what changes, if any, are necessary.

Tips for Using Activities at Individual Stations at Family Meetings

Listed below are suggestions to make activities at individual stations and rotations from station to station go smoothly.

- Ask a staff member or volunteer to be at each station to provide families assistance, as needed.
- Write down and post step-by-step procedures to be followed at each station for easy reference.
- Identify stations by colors or symbols related to meeting themes so families will be able to locate them easily.
- Alert families at least two minutes prior to station rotation. This will allow time to clean up and prepare for the next group.
- Use an attention-getting signal to notify families when it is time to rotate. Possible signals include a bell, music, flicking lights, or a whistle.
- Ask participants to rotate from one station to the next in a clockwise direction.
- Initiate station rotation every 15-20 minutes to keep the meeting moving.
- If stations are located in separate rooms or outdoors, be in contact with the person directing the station to stay on the same time schedule.

References
(Jones, J. 1989). *Changing needs for a changing future*. Keynote address June 14, Austin, TX. New York: National Center for Children in Poverty.

Family Meetings

Are You Hungry for Family Fun?

Come Join the Fun!

We will have fun activities to satisfy your cravings. Bring your appetite and join us for activities based on Eric Carle's book *The Very Hungry Caterpillar*! You'll learn how children's literature can be integrated into daily curriculum activties.

Date _____

Time _____

Place _____

Who's Invited: The whole family

Dress for fun!

Refreshments will be served.

Please complete and detach the form below by _____ so we can reserve a space for your family.

- -

_____ Yes, we will attend the "Are You Hungry for Fun?" family meeting.
_____ Sorry, we will be unable to attend the meeting.

Child's name _____

Number of adults attending _____ Number of children attending _____

If you have any questions or need transportation, please call
_____.

Name _____ Phone _____

Email address _____

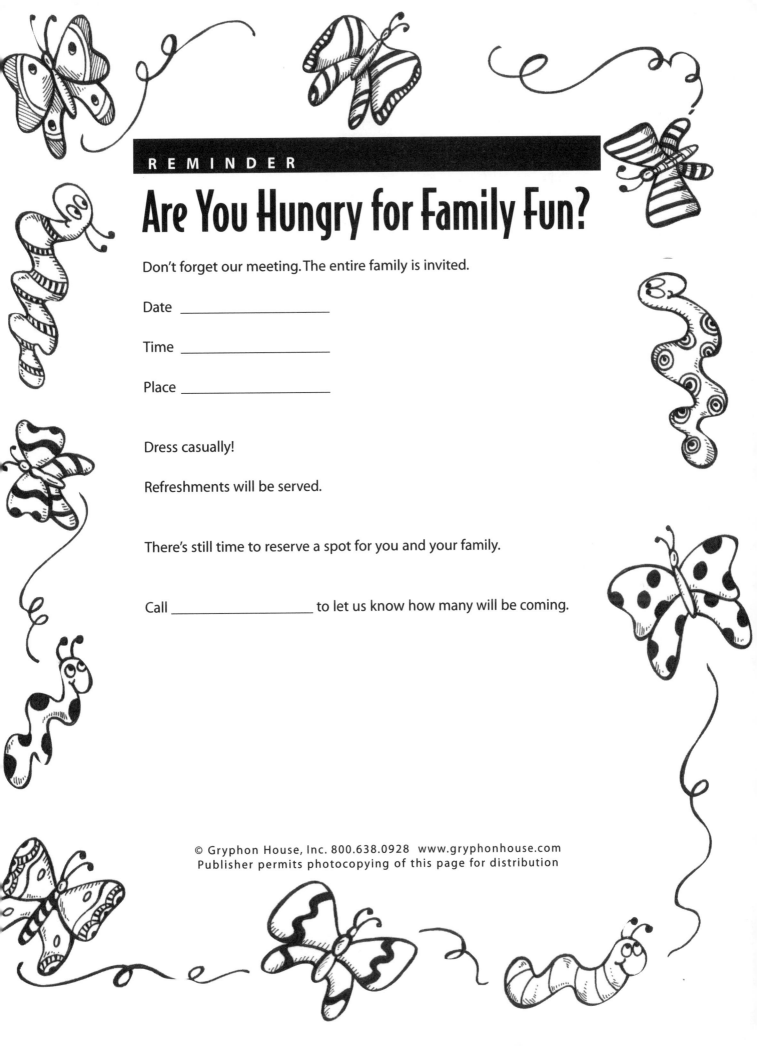

Are You Hungry for Family Fun?

Don't forget our meeting. The entire family is invited.

Date _____

Time _____

Place _____

Dress casually!

Refreshments will be served.

There's still time to reserve a spot for you and your family.

Call _____ to let us know how many will be coming.

Content Areas
Art
Literacy
Math
Motor Skills
Science

Purpose
To demonstrate how children's literature can be integrated into daily curricular activities.

Nametags

Materials
Red, yellow, green, and orange construction paper
Scissors
Butterfly pattern
Markers

- Use the butterfly pattern below to make nametags in four colors.
- Assign one color per family.
- The different colored nametags will be used to assign families to one of four activity stations.
- Make an extra set of nametags in each of the four colors to post at the activity stations.

Mixer—Apple Matching

- As families arrive, distribute the butterfly nametags.
- Ask each family member to write his or her name on the butterfly and use masking tape to attach it to his or her clothing.
- Be sure that all members of each family have the same color nametag so they will work together at each activity station.
- After all of the families have arrived, give each family one half of an apple puzzle (see illustration below).
- Ask them to move about the room and interact with other families while trying to find the matching half of their apple puzzle.
- When they find the matching half, they must learn two things about the other family—the names of the people in the family and the title of a book they have most recently read to their child/children.
- After everyone gathers these two pieces of information, bring the whole group together and ask one person from each family to introduce their "matching" family.

Introduction

In this meeting, families learn how literacy, science, art, math, and motor skills—essential components of an early childhood curriculum—can be enhanced with the reading of a favorite children's story, Eric Carle's *The Very Hungry Caterpillar*.

Read aloud Eric Carle's *The Very Hungry Caterpillar*. For greater effect, read from a big book and act out the story with a puppet, if available. After reading the story ask families to go to an activity station that is designated by a color that corresponds to their nametag. The four activity stations are:

1. Flitter Flutter (red)
2. Caterpillar Crawl (yellow)
3. Watercolor Butterfly (green)
4. Caterpillar Counting and Snacking (orange)

Families move clockwise from the first activity station to the next when room lights are turned off and on.

Family Meeting Activities

Station #1: Flitter Flutter: The Life Cycle of a Butterfly (designated by a red caterpillar)

Visualize the four stages of the life cycle of a butterfly.

Materials
Paper plates
Glue
Navy beans
Precut leaves made from green construction paper
Small green, yellow, and red pompoms
Cotton balls
Coffee filters
Crayons (variety of colors)
Spring clothespins
Collection of small tree twigs (3" long)
Poster board with the directions written on it (see next page)
Samples of finished product
Brown washable markers

What to Do

(Demonstrate a finished product and assist families as needed.)

1. Use a black crayon to mark four equal sections on the paper plate. Number each section from 1-4.
2. Glue paper leaf to section 1 of the plate.
3. Glue navy bean (egg) on paper leaf.
4. Glue three pompoms to section 2 of the plate and mark legs with crayons, as illustrated.
5. Glue twig to section 3 of the paper plate.
6. Use brown washable marker to partially color the cotton ball.
7. Wrap and glue a cotton ball on a stick to make a chrysalis.
8. Color the coffee filter with different colors using crayons.
9. Gather the colored coffee filter and clip with clothespin.
10. Talk about the life cycle of the caterpillar.

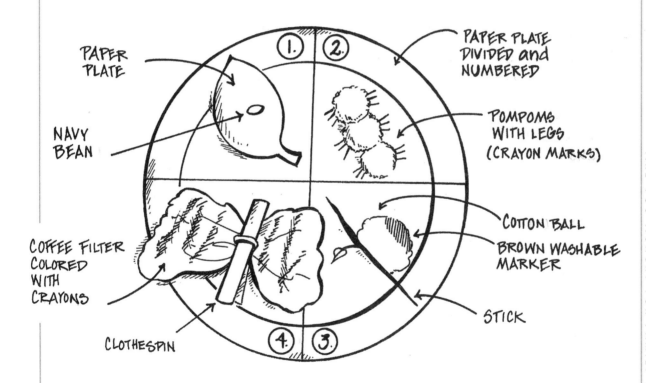

PAPER PLATE

PAPER PLATE DIVIDED and NUMBERED

NAVY BEAN

POMPOMS WITH LEGS (CRAYON MARKS)

COTTON BALL

BROWN WASHABLE MARKER

COFFEE FILTER COLORED WITH CRAYONS

STICK

CLOTHESPIN

Station #2: Caterpillar Crawl

(yellow caterpillar nametag)

Develop the locomotion skill of crawling.

Materials
Large rug

What to Do
1. As a group, talk about how a caterpillar moves by using all of its muscles together, slowly and smoothly.
2. Slowly move one finger on the rug as a caterpillar would. Caterpillars move carefully, with no one bumping into another person.
3. Move together as a group. Do the "Caterpillar Crawl" by kneeling on the rug in a straight line and then swaying together. Sway slowly. Sway fast!
4. Move together in different positions! Suggest new ways to move together.

Inspired by "Caterpillar Crawl" on page 30 of *The Busy Classroom* by Patty Claycomb.

Station #3: Watercolor Butterfly

(green caterpillar nametag)

Increase children's sensitivity to color, color mixtures, and color combinations.

Materials
Watercolor paints
Paintbrushes
Butterfly patterns made of pre-cut white construction paper (see pattern on next page)
Paint shirts
Area to dry paintings
Photos of butterflies

What to Do
1. Talk about butterflies, pointing out all the beautiful colors on their wings.
2. Look at photos of butterflies.
3. Paint the pre-cut butterflies using many colors of watercolor paints.

ARE YOU HUNGRY FOR FAMILY FUN?

27

Station #4: Caterpillar Counting and Snacking (orange caterpillar nametag)

Develop number recognition, number correspondence, and counting skills while creating an enjoyable healthy snack.

Materials
6 three-ounce paper cups for each family
Markers
Crayons
Paper clips
Small brads
Cubes of apples, pears, plums, strawberries, oranges
The Very Hungry Caterpillar by Eric Carle

What to Do
(Set up a model for participants to emulate.)
1. Write the numbers 1-5 on each of five cups.
2. Turn the sixth cup upside down and decorate it with facial features.
3. Line a set of empty cups in order 1 through 6 for your child.
4. Connect cups 1-5 with paper clips.
5. Turn the sixth cup upside down and attach it with a small brad.
6. The caterpillar had the right idea when he filled up on fruit Monday through Friday! Ask your child how many of each fruit the Very Hungry Caterpillar ate. Have the book handy to refer to as your child counts one apple piece, two pear slices, three plum pieces, four strawberry pieces, and five orange pieces.
7. Fill the cups with the appropriate fruit and number.
8. Eat the fruit snack now or later.

Thank everyone for coming and invite them to share a snack of seasonal fruit and crackers after completing an evaluation form.

Are You Hungry for Family Fun?

Family Meeting Evaluation

We would like to know what you thought about the "Are You Hungry for Family Fun?" family meeting. Please circle the picture that best describes your feelings. We appreciate your feedback, so please feel free to make comments. Thank you.

Never hatched   Inched along   Really flew

Comments and Suggestions

_____

_____

_____

_____

_____

_____

_____

_____

Thank you for coming!

INVITATION

Bananas About Books

Come to our family meeting!

Date _____

Time _____

Place _____

Who's Invited: The Whole Family

Develop literacy materials that you can use at home with your child.

Dress for fun! Refreshments will be served.

We need supplies for our "Bananas about Books" family meeting. Please help us by sending in any of the following:

- a small photo of your child
- cereal boxes
- magazines

- fabric scraps
- aluminum foil
- yarn

- sandpaper
- cotton balls
- birdseed

Thanks for anything you can send!

Please complete and detach the form below by _____ so we can reserve a space for your family.

- -

_____ Yes, we will attend the "Bananas about Books" family meeting.
_____ Sorry, we will be unable to attend the meeting.

Child's name _____

Number of adults attending _____ Number of children attending _____

If you have any questions or need transportation, please call _____.

Name _____ Phone _____
Email address _____

REMINDER

Bananas About Books

Don't forget our meeting! The entire family is invited.

Date _____

Time _____

Place _____

Dress casually!

Refreshments will be served.

There is still time to reserve a spot for you and your family.

Call _____ to let us know how many will be coming.

Content Areas

Literacy
Motor Skills
Social Development

Purpose

To create a sense of partnership while developing materials that can be used at home to foster literacy experiences for children.

Related Books

Here Comes Mother Goose by Iona Opie
My Very First Mother Goose by Iona Opie

Nametags

Materials
Banana-shaped nametags (see illustration on the next page) in four colors (yellow, green, brown, and red)
Markers
Masking tape

- As families arrive, give each a nametag.
- Ask them to print their name on a nametag and use the masking tape to attach the nametag to their clothing.
- Be sure to give all members of each family the same color nametag so they can stay together as they rotate to the four activity stations.
- Make an extra set of nametags in each of the four colors to post at activity stations.

NAME:

NAME:

NAME:

NAME:

BANANAS ABOUT BOOKS

Mixer

Materials
Tape or compact disc player
Nursery rhyme background music
Masking tape
3" x 5" index cards

- As families, arrive distribute the nametags.
- Ask them to stand and form a large circle facing the center of the room.
- Use the masking tape to attach a 3" x 5" index card labeled with the name of a nursery rhyme character to each participant's back. Suggested characters include Little Boy Blue, Humpty Dumpty, Little Bo Peep, Mary (Had a Little Lamb), Mary (Mary Quite Contrary), Jack and Jill, Wee Willie Winkle, Old Woman in a Shoe, Old King Cole, Pussy Cat, and Little Jack Horner.
- Tell participants that they now have the name of a nursery rhyme character on their backs. They must guess who that character is. There is only one rule: You may ask the other participants only yes or no questions to discover the name of your character. Families can stay together and assist their children, as needed.
- If desired, softly play some nursery rhyme background music as participants mix and ask questions of one another.
- After about 10 minutes stop the music and ask everyone to be seated. Ask each participant if he or she discovered the name of his or her character.

Introduction

Books written by children help them see connections between spoken and written words. At this family meeting, children will be able to create their own books that may be based on their interests, and can be done at home. Attitudes young children hold about books are greatly influenced by what they see modeled at home. Read, read, read—not only to children, but for yourself as well. So, let's get "bananas about books" both at school and at home!

Tell the families that there are four activity stations. Each station is color-coded with a yellow, red, brown, or green banana. Ask the families to check the color of their banana nametag and go to the appropriate activity station at this time.

1. Cereal Box Book (yellow)
2. Look and Touch Book (green)
3. An Accordion Book (red)
4. A Reading Necklace (brown)

The families will proceed clockwise to the next activity station when they hear the "Day O" song being played.

Family Meeting Activities

Station #1: Cereal Box Book

(yellow banana nametag)

This activity demonstrates that children can read environmental print, which is an excellent early reading activity that can be done at home.

Materials
Variety of cereal boxes
Yarn
Paper punch
Scissors

What to Do
1. Choose your favorite cereals and cut out the front and back of the boxes.
2. Use a paper punch to make holes in the top left and lower left of the box. Use the holes in the first punched box as a pattern for the remaining boxes.
3. Pull yarn through the holes and tie.
4. Now you have a cereal book! Read it. Take it home and read it again.
5. Make other books at home using box fronts such as macaroni and cheese, crackers, and other boxes.

Station #2: Look and Touch Book

(green banana nametag)

The activity on the following page is a simple way to incorporate the sense of touch and shape recognition into an easy-to-read book.

Materials
Paper
Stapler
Glue
Crayons
Cotton balls
Sandpaper
Aluminum foil
Cloth scraps
Foam plates or meat trays
Birdseed
Tile squares
Tagboard shape patterns (four of each shape—circle, square, and triangle)
Tape
Poster board
Markers

What to Do
1. Fold two pieces of paper in half. Staple the folded paper together to create an eight-page book.
2. Use a crayon to print "Look and Touch Book by (child's name)" on the cover page and to number the inner pages 1-6.
3. Use the square shape pattern to trace a square on each of the first two pages. Use the circle pattern to trace a circle on each of the middle two pages. Use the triangle pattern to trace a triangle on each of the last two pages.
4. Glue a cotton square to the first page and use a crayon or marker to print "a soft square" on that page. Glue or tape a tile square onto the second page and print a "hard square" on that page.
5. Cut out and glue a sandpaper circle to the third page and print "a rough circle" on that page. Cut out and glue a foam circle to the fourth page and print "a smooth circle" on that page.
6. Glue birdseed on the fifth page and print "a bumpy triangle" on that page. Cut out and glue a triangle of aluminum foil to the sixth page and print "a slick triangle" on that page.
7. Take the book home and read it with your child.

Station #3: An Accordion Book

(red banana nametag)

An excellent way to develop number recognition and sequencing skills.

Materials
Markers
Scissors
Glue
Paper
Index cards
Poster board (to write the following instructions for families at this station)

What to Do
1. Fold a sheet of 8 ½" x 11" paper the long way. Cut in half along the fold.
2. Tape the two strips of paper together on the front and back sides.
3. Fold like an accordion into eight sections.
4. Cut an index card into two pieces and glue one piece on the front of the first section and another piece to the back of the last section to serve as a cover.
5. Use a marker to print the book title, such as "Numbers" or "My Counting Book."
6. Use the markers to write the word "one" on the first fold. Also make one dot or a mark of your choice. Follow the same procedure with numbers one through eight, putting only one number on each fold.
7. Use this approach at home with photos of your child. Start with a newborn photo on the first fold and show the growth of your child with photos taken from birth to present. Another idea that shows the sequence of events in order is to plant some grass seed or a flower and ask your child to draw pictures on each fold from day (or week) one through day (or week) eight, showing the stages of growth.

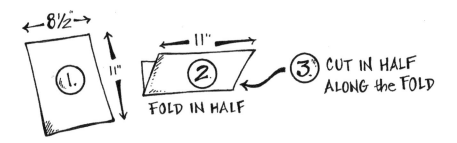

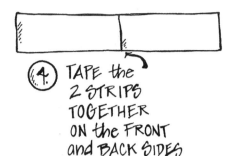

④ TAPE the 2 STRIPS TOGETHER ON the FRONT and BACK SIDES

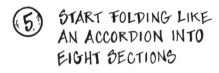

⑤ START FOLDING LIKE AN ACCORDION INTO EIGHT SECTIONS

⑥ ATTACH ½ AN INDEX CARD to the FRONT and BACK (WILL BE the COVERS)

⑦ TITLE the BOOK: "NUMBERS" -or- "MY COUNTING BOOK" or ANYTHING YOU WISH !

Station #4: A Reading Necklace

(brown banana nametag)

This activity helps the child attach meaning to words.

Materials
Markers or crayons
Index cards
Paper punch
Yarn in a variety of colors
Small photo of the child (ask for these in advance or take individual
photos of the children attending the center and have them available for
this activity)

What to Do
1. Glue your child's photo on an index card.
2. Print the child's name below the photo.
3. Print your child's age on another card.
4. Write the name of your child's favorite color on another card. Let your
child select the color of the crayon you use to print.
5. At home, make a necklace of the child's favorite foods using photos of
foods cut from magazines.

Thank everyone for coming and invite them to share a snack of seasonal
fruit and crackers.

Bananas About Books

Family Meeting Evaluation

How ap"peel"ing was this meeting?

A bunch   Did we slip?

Comments and Suggestions

_____

_____

_____

_____

_____

_____

_____

Thank you for coming!

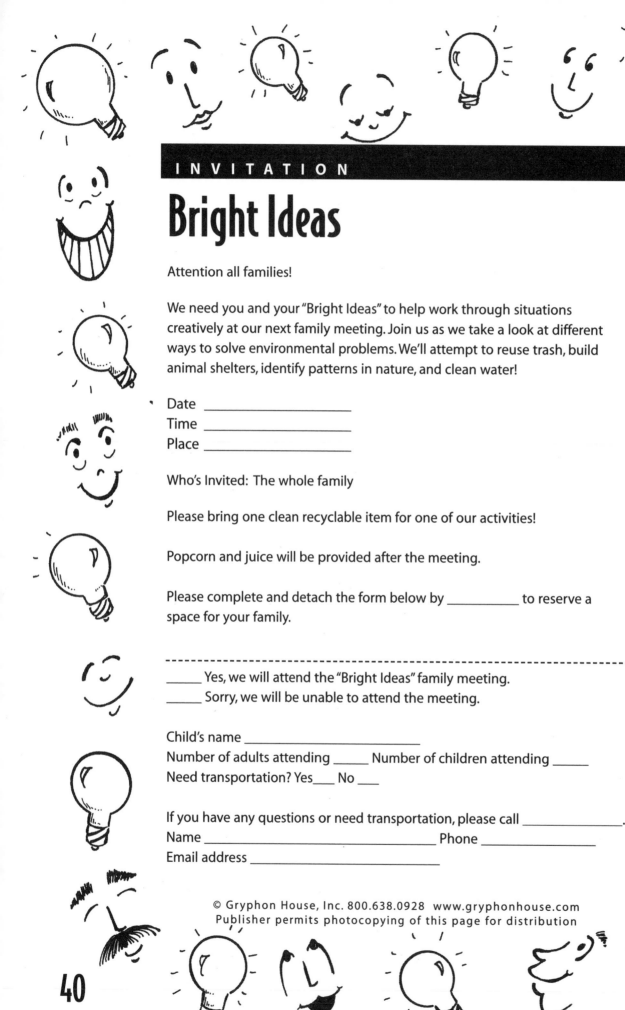

Bright Ideas

Attention all families!

We need you and your "Bright Ideas" to help work through situations creatively at our next family meeting. Join us as we take a look at different ways to solve environmental problems. We'll attempt to reuse trash, build animal shelters, identify patterns in nature, and clean water!

Date _____

Time _____

Place _____

Who's Invited: The whole family

Please bring one clean recyclable item for one of our activities!

Popcorn and juice will be provided after the meeting.

Please complete and detach the form below by _____ to reserve a space for your family.

_____ Yes, we will attend the "Bright Ideas" family meeting.
_____ Sorry, we will be unable to attend the meeting.

Child's name _____
Number of adults attending _____ Number of children attending _____
Need transportation? Yes___ No ___

If you have any questions or need transportation, please call _____.
Name _____ Phone _____
Email address _____

Bright Ideas

Just a Reminder...

The "Bright Ideas" family meeting will be:

Date _____

Time _____

Place _____

Please call _____ immediately if you still need to RSVP.

We would love to see you!

Content Areas
Math
Problem Solving
Science
Social Development
Social Studies

Purpose
To encourage families to recognize problems and learn to work through them together.

Related Books
A Chair for My Mother by Vera B. Williams
Joseph Had a Little Overcoat by Simms Taback
Somewhere Today by Shelley Moore Thomas

Nametags

Materials
Construction paper
Scissors
Masking tape
Pencils
Markers

- Use the patterns of a mouse face, a leaf, a water drop, and a trashcan (see next page) to make nametags.
- Assign one design per family.
- The different shaped nametags will be used to assign families to one of four activity stations.
- Make an extra set of nametags in each of the four shapes to post at the activity stations.

Mixer

Materials
Index cards (two per person)
Markers

- As people write their names on nametags, give them two index cards so they can write the first letter of their first name on one card, and the first letter of their last name on the other card.
- Be sure all members of each family have the same shape nametag so they will work together at each activity station.
- Ask the families to go to the station with the same design as their nametag.
- Once everyone is at their beginning station, the group should use the letter cards to make words. They can make one or more words, but they should try to use all of the letters if possible.
- After about 10 minutes, ask the groups to share the words they made. If some groups were not able to create a word, ask the other groups if they can help create a word from the letters.
- Congratulate the families on completing their first problem-solving activity of the evening successfully!

Introduction

Our fast-paced world is home to fast-food restaurants and microwave ovens that provide meals in minutes. Our modes of transportation enable us to travel anywhere within our country within a few hours or to the other side of the world in less than a day. And if that isn't enough, computers have given us the capability to send information instantly and to communicate with people anywhere in the world. While the benefits of progress are numerous, it has also led us to look for, and expect, instant gratification. We sometimes forget that we need to take time to work through problems and situations to solve them responsibly.

The activities at tonight's family meeting provide opportunities to solve problems creatively. It may take more than one attempt, and it will likely require teamwork. But, problems aren't always solved instantly, and many of life's most memorable lessons come after we make mistakes and work to correct them.

The nametags correspond to the activity stations where families begin. If a family has a mouse nametag, they begin at the station with the mouse displayed. If a family has a water drop, they begin at the station with the water drop displayed, and so on. The four activity stations are:

1. Mouse House (mouse)
2. Trash Town (trash can)
3. Water Treatment (water drop)
4. Patterns (leaf)

Families move clockwise from the first activity station to the next when room lights are turned off and on.

Family Meeting Activities

Station #1: Mouse House

(mouse nametag)

All living creatures need safe shelter to survive. This activity is a challenge to create a shelter that will keep an "animal" dry.

Materials
Kits for each family containing:
> 2" pompom to represent a mouse; add facial features and a tail if desired
> 6" x 6" piece of plastic (use plastic bags from cleaners)
> 4 straws
> One 6" piece of masking tape
> One manila folder
> 12" piece of yarn
> 12 strips of construction paper ($\frac{1}{2}$" x 12")

One tennis ball
Watering can with water
Container to catch water (water table or 13" x 9" cake pan)

What to Do
1. Each family takes one pre-assembled kit. The pompom in the bag represents a mouse.
2. Using only the materials in the kit, build a shelter to protect your mouse from a falling object (represented by the tennis ball) and rain (water from a sprinkle can). Fold, tear, or bend any of the materials, but do not use glue or scissors.
3. Once your mouse house is constructed, place the "mouse" inside the house.

4. Now see if the house can withstand the elements! Ask a family member to hold the tennis ball above your mouse house. Release the ball and see if the house protects the mouse.

5. Next, place the house in the water table or cake pan. Ask another family member to sprinkle water from the watering can over the house. Did it keep the mouse dry?

6. Share your house designs and their results with the rest of the group at the activity station. What worked best? What improvements would you make next time?

Station #2: Trash Town

(trash can nametag)

Reusing items instead of throwing them away can help protect our environment. This activity provides an opportunity to work cooperatively while contributing to a clean planet.

Materials
Recyclable items brought from home
Scissors
Tape
Stapler
Pencils
Paint
Paintbrushes
Newspaper (to cover work area)
Tub of water for paint clean up
Paper towels

What to Do
1. Use the clean recyclable items you brought from home to design a structure for a group display. Design structures related to ongoing class themes, such as the zoo, the community, the park, airport, or any other theme.
2. Make your own structures or work with other families at the station. Use any of the materials listed above for the construction.
3. Once the structures are finished, arrange them in a common area so the other groups can add their structures as they are completed.

Station #3: Water Treatment

(water drop nametag)

This activity is a problem-solving challenge: create a water filter system that will successfully clean muddy water.

Materials

Jar of muddy water
Sifter
Sand
Cotton balls
Small pebbles or gravel
Two plastic tubs
Paper towels for cleanup

What to Do

The jar of muddy water represents a sample from a pond that is polluted. The families at this station pretend they are environmentalists who have been given the responsibility to clean up the muddy water.

1. Work as a group to create a water treatment plant from the materials listed above to see if you can get the water clean.
2. Try again if your first attempt did not get the water clean.
3. If you cannot get the water clean before it is time to rotate to another station, do not be discouraged. Maybe another group will devise an effective water treatment plant!
4. If the water came through fairly clean, discuss why your design worked.
5. Pour the water through your treatment system more than once if time permits.
6. If none of the groups successfully cleaned the water, quickly assemble an effective model by layering the items in the sifter as follows: cotton on the bottom layer, sand in the middle, and gravel on the top layer. Pour muddy water through and watch what happens!

Station #4: Patterns

(leaf nametag)

Identify patterns in nature and create new patterns using a variety of nature items.

Materials
Items from nature that exhibit patterns (leaves, flowers, shells, acorns)
Hand lenses
Crayons or markers
White construction paper (9" x 12")

What to Do
1. Look for and identify patterns in the items found in nature. Use hand lenses to look for small details. Share your findings with others at the station.
2. Take turns making patterns using the nature items. Begin with simple patterns, increasing the difficulty only after your child has successfully identified the less difficult patterns. For example, display the following pattern: leaf, flower, shell; leaf, flower, shell. Ask your child what comes next and let him or her continue the pattern.
3. After the children have created and recognized patterns, encourage them to make their own patterns by drawing patterns on paper with crayons or markers.
4. Ask the children to share their patterns with each other, if time permits.
5. Clean up the station so it is ready for the next group.

Thank everyone for coming and invite them to share a snack of popcorn and juice.

EVALUATION

Bright Ideas

Family Meeting Evaluation

Please tell us what you thought of tonight's meeting. Please circle the picture that represents how you felt about our meeting. Feel free to add any additional remarks.

Thank you for your help!

I feel happy and bright about the meeting. It was great!

The meeting was okay, but it could have been brighter.

The meeting was dull and did not shed much light.

Comments and Suggestions

_____

_____

_____

_____

_____

_____

Thank you for coming!

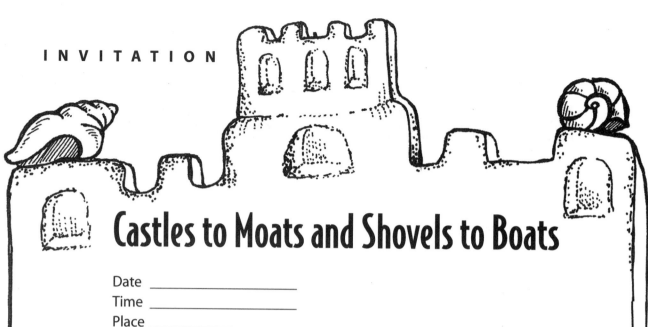

Castles to Moats and Shovels to Boats

Date _____

Time _____

Place _____

Come one, come all
to a night that's grand,
Come do what you can
with water and sand!

You can build a boat
and see if it floats,
Make a castle without
much hassle.

Fill jars with sand
and write a letter.
For an evening of fun,
it doesn't get better.

Grab your flip-flops,
shovel, and pail,
head for _____
to make your boat sail!

Who's Invited: The whole family
Dress appropriately for an evening of sand and water fun!
Refreshments will be served.

Please detach and return the form below by _____ or call
_____ to reserve a place for your family.

____Yes, we will attend the "Castles to Moats and Shovels to Boats" family
meeting.
_____ No, we can't attend.

Child's name _____

Number of adults attending _____ Number of children attending _____

Need transportation? Yes___ No ___

If you have questions or need transportation, please call _____.

Name _____ Phone _____

Email address _____

REMINDER

Castles to Moats and Shovels to Boats

Just a reminder!

Our "Castles to Moats and Shovels to Boats" family meeting is quickly approaching.

Date _____

Time _____

Place _____

Who's Invited: The whole family

Remember, we will be using water, sand, and food coloring, so please dress accordingly!

Refreshments will be provided.

If you have not responded yet, please call _____ as soon as possible so we will have plenty of supplies on hand.

Thank you!

Content Areas

Literacy
Motor Skills
Problem Solving
Sand and Water
Social Development

Purpose

To develop gross and fine motor skills, to explore creative uses of sand and water, and to interact with others cooperatively.

Nametags

Materials
Red, yellow, green, and orange construction paper
Masking tape
Pencils
Markers

- Use the patterns (see next page) to make nametags.
- Assign one shape per family.
- Use the different shaped nametags to assign families to one of five activity stations.
- Make an extra set of nametags in each of the five shapes to post at the activity stations.

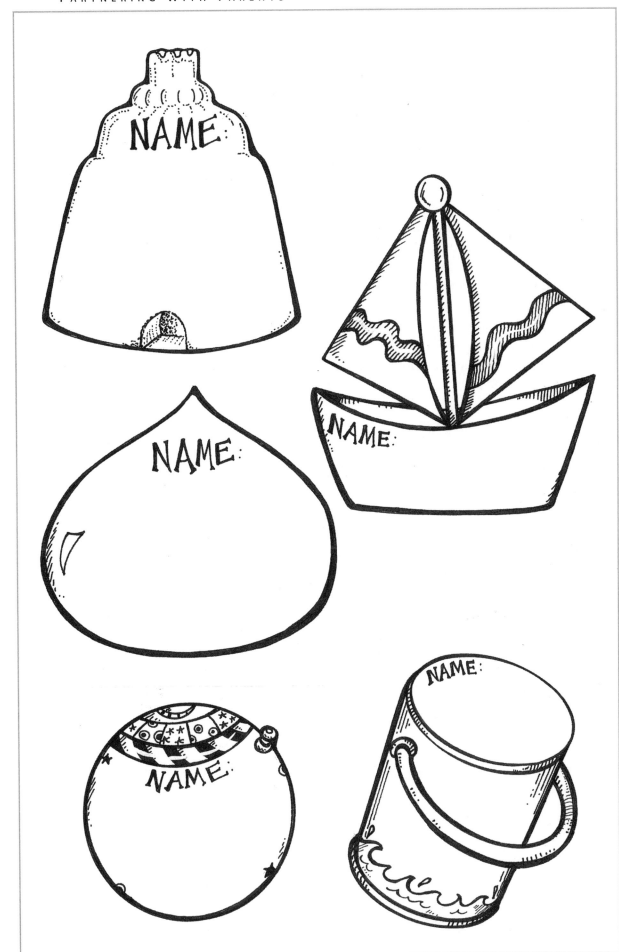

NAME:

NAME:

NAME:

NAME:

NAME:

Castles to Moats and Shovels to Boats

Mixer

- As families arrive, distribute the shape nametags.
- Ask each family member to write his or her name on one of the shapes and use masking tape to attach it to his or her clothing.
- Be sure all members of each family have the same shape nametag so they will work together at each activity station.
- Ask the group to form a large circle.
- Stand in the middle of the circle holding a beach ball. Introduce yourself by saying, "Hi, my name is _____. I'm your child's teacher. The parent I throw the ball to will step to the middle of the circle and introduce him- or herself by saying his or her name and giving his or her child's name. Then, that parent will throw the ball to another parent who will follow the same procedure. We will continue throwing the ball until all the adults have introduced themselves." Before tossing the ball, look at the parent to whom you are throwing the ball and say, "I'm throwing the ball to you."

Introduction

Tonight's activities offer opportunities for playing, discovering, and learning with sand and water. Activities will explore number relationships, develop social awareness, and challenge the group to use their imaginations to create sand and water designs. Activities also include the use of both fine and gross motor skills.

The shape of the nametags designates the beginning activity station for families. The activity stations are:

1. Sand Land (sandcastle)
2. Sand Writing (beach ball)
3. Rainbow in a Jar (sand bucket)
4. Colorful Water Works (water drop)
5. Float-a-Boat (boat)

Families will have a few minutes to clean up when they hear a bell. (Ring the bell loud enough so they can hear.) They will rotate clockwise to the next activity station when they hear the song "Row, Row, Row Your Boat."

Family Meeting Activities

Station #1: Sand Land

(sandcastle nametag)

Explore number relationships by creating sandcastles with a variety of features. To develop social awareness, build a neighborhood of castles by adding roads and moats connecting to other participants' castles.

Materials
Sand table or plastic pool
Sand
Water
Variety of containers to use as molds, such as buckets, plastic shoeboxes, butter tubs, paper cups, cylinders
Items to decorate the castle, such as buttons, shells, plastic bottle caps
Plastic spoons
Shovels
Plastic figures (people, animals, boats, and so on)

What to Do
1. Begin by making a base for your castle in any shape or size. Use a mold or just form a base using your hands.
2. Do one of the following or create your own ideas: Make your castle larger by using three molds. Add two towers to your castle. Add one window to your castle.
3. After all the castles are complete, make roads and moats connecting the castles to create a "royal kingdom."
4. Let the children play in the castles using plastic figures.

Station #2: Sand Writing

(beach ball nametag)

Develop fine motor skills by creating colorful letters with glue and colored sand.

Materials
Aluminum foil trays
Colored sand
Bottled glue
Index cards with letters and numbers written on them
Blank index cards

What to Do

Prepare the colored sand in advance. Keep colors separate by placing sand in aluminum foil trays. Have several trays of each color available.

1. Select a card with a number or letter.
2. Cover the letter or number with glue.
3. Sprinkle colored sand over the card.
4. Shake off the excess sand and let it dry.
5. Create your own design using a blank card.

Note: Two of the stations at this family meeting call for colored sand. For extra fun, let the children help make the colored sand a few days before the family meeting.

Recipe for Colored Sand
Mix 1 cup of white sand with 1 tablespoon of powdered tempera paint. The colors should be bold. If not, add more tempera paint, a small amount at a time, until the desired color is achieved.

Station #3: Rainbow in a Jar

(sand bucket nametag)

Experiment with layering and arranging varieties of colored sand in a jar. This make-it and take-it activity lets everyone create a colorful jar to take home, and it develops fine motor skills.

Materials
Baby food jars (one per person)
Colored sand
Funnels
Spoons
Straws
Cotton swabs
Permanent markers (adults only)

What to Do

1. Write your name (or a family member's name) in permanent marker on top of the jar lid.
2. Help your child use a spoon and funnel to scoop a small amount of colored sand into the jar. Experiment by arranging the sand using a cotton swab or blowing gently with a straw.
3. Add another layer of a different color of sand. Repeat this process until the jar is full.
4. Screw the lid on the jar tightly. Do not shake the jars!

Station #4: Colorful Water Works

(water drop nametag)

Experiment with colors, creating standard colors with food coloring and additional colors by mixing a variety of colors.

Materials
Little Blue and Little Yellow by Leo Lionni
Water
Plastic tubs for holding water
Food coloring (blue, red, yellow, and green)
See-through containers
Plastic spoons
Funnels
Paper towels
Color Creations handout (see page 60)
Crayons

What to Do
1. One adult reads *Little Blue and Little Yellow* by Leo Lionni to the group.
2. Each family fills four see-through containers with water. Add food coloring to each container to make the following colors: blue, red, yellow, and green.
3. Create a variety of colors by adding different food coloring to the containers of colored water. For example, add red food coloring to the container of yellow water. What color does it make? Add blue food coloring to the red water. What happens?
4. Ask children to use crayons to record his or her discoveries on their Color Creations paper (see form on page 60). Make a mark on each line to show which colors were used and which colors were created.
5. After you finish mixing colors, empty the containers into a tub so they are ready for the next group.

Station #5: Float-a-Boat

(boat nametag)

Work together to create a boat that will float. Once you have succeeded, test the boat to see if it is unsinkable!

Materials
Aluminum foil
Wooden blocks
Styrofoam trays
Clay
Colored construction paper for sails
Straws
Washers
Sand and water table or plastic dishpans
Water

What to Do
1. Work together as a family to create a boat that will float. Use any of the materials.
2. Once you have made a boat that floats, see if your boat will stay afloat when weight is added. Place washers on your boat, one at a time, to see if the boat is unsinkable.
3. Build additional boats using other materials. See if the new boats stay afloat or sink as you add washers. Did one boat sink faster than the other? Did any of the boats stay afloat?
4. Ask the other families at this station to share experiences and results.

Thank everyone for coming and invite them to share a snack of seasonal fruit and crackers.

EVALUATION

Castles to Moats and Shovel to Boats

Family Meeting Evaluation

Please let us know what you thought of the meeting by marking the banner that best describes your reaction to our meeting. Thank you for your opinion!

Comments and Suggestions

_____
_____
_____
_____
_____
_____

Thank you for coming!

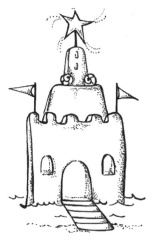

Color Creations

By _____

_____ + _____ = _____

_____ + _____ = _____

_____ + _____ = _____

_____ + _____ = _____

Keep track of your findings on this sheet. Use crayons to indicate the colors you used and the colors you made.

INVITATION

Come and See Whoo's Outside

Come and See Whoo's in Your Backyard

Share outdoor fun with your child!

Date _____
Time _____
Place _____

Who's Invited: The whole family

Dress for fun!

Refreshments will be served.

Please complete and detach the form below by _____ to reserve a space for your family.

_____ Yes, we will attend the "Come and See Whoo's Outside"
        family meeting.
_____ Sorry, we are unable to attend the meeting.

Child's name _____
Number of adults attending _____ Number of children attending _____

If you have questions or need transportation, please call _____.

Name _____ Phone _____
Email address _____

REMINDER

Come and See Whoo's Outside

**Don't forget to attend this workshop
about outdoor learning experiences.**

Whoo's in Your Backyard?

Date _____

Time _____

Place _____

Who's Invited: The whole family

Dress for fun!

Refreshments will be served.

Any Questions? Call _____

Content Areas
Art
Language
Math
Outdoors
Science

Purpose
To share with families some developmentally appropriate outdoor learning experiences that they can share with their children in their own backyards or in any outdoor setting. (This family meeting is best done in late spring or early fall.)

Nametags

Materials
Construction paper in red, green, yellow, and blue
Wise old owl pattern (see below)
Markers or crayons

- Cut construction paper into owl shapes using the owl pattern (see pattern at right).
- Different colored nametags will be used to assign families to one of four activity stations.
- Make an extra set of nametags in each of the four colors to post at the activity stations.

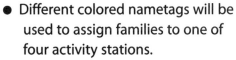

Come and See Whoo's Outside

Mixer—Super Outdoor Lookers

Materials
Enlarged photographs of outdoor areas and structures, cut into four puzzle sections

- As families arrive, distribute the nametags.
- Ask each family member to write his or her name on the nametag and use masking tape to attach it to clothing.
- Be sure all members of each family have the same color nametag so they will work together at each activity station.
- Give each family a portion of a photo.
- Tell them that they have been given part of a photograph of something in the school or center outdoor area.
- Ask them to explore the outdoor area to find the item.
- Once they find the area, they are to introduce themselves to the other families.
- Families then piece together the four pieces of the photo to check their accuracy.

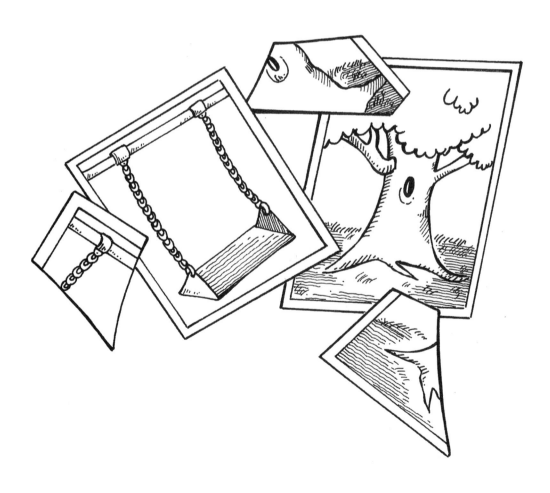

Introduction

Children love to be outdoors and are excited about their outdoor discoveries. Activities in this family meeting give families the opportunity to join their child(ren) in outdoor activities that are sure to enhance, and possibly rekindle, the excitement that comes from the joy of outdoor discovery.

Families proceed to the outdoor activity station with the colored owl that matches their nametag. The four activity stations are:

1. Rubbings (yellow owl)
2. Outdoor Shadows (red owl)
3. Texture Hunt (blue owl)
4. Color Tally Cards (green owl)

Families move clockwise to the next activity station when they hear the bell.

Family Meeting Activities

Station #1: Rubbings (yellow owl nametag)

There are many textures outdoors that can be used to create a variety of interesting designs and patterns. The opportunity to create a one-of-a-kind backyard mural is a worthwhile activity that the entire family can enjoy.

Materials
Large crayons with paper wrapping removed
Pieces of 8" x 18" white cloth (can be torn from old sheets)

What to Do
1. Take one piece of cloth and an assortment of crayons.
2. Explore the outdoors to find as many items as possible to use for rubbings, such as leaves, tree bark, grass, stones, sand, twigs, flowers, logs, feathers, playground equipment, boards, and concrete surfaces.
3. To make a rubbing, one person holds the fabric tight against the object and another person rubs the crayon sideways until a pattern appears.
4. After the rubbings are finished, parents return to the yellow activity station to share rubbing collections with other families at this station.

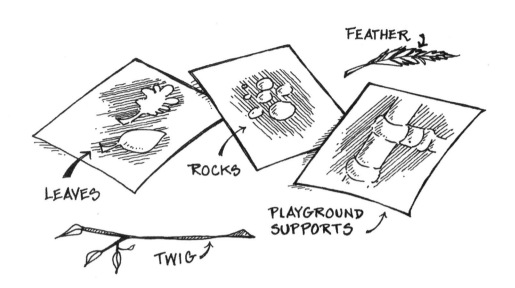

Station #2: Outdoor Shadows

(red owl nametag)

Light travels through the air in straight lines. Shadows are created by anything that comes between the light source—the sun—and the background surface.

Materials
Paper
Pencil

What to Do
1. Take a sheet of paper and a pencil.
2. Search the outdoor area to identify and list on the paper the number of shadows you discover. These might be shadows that are cast by playground equipment, trees, bushes, fences, and so on.
3. After you have completed your list, return to the red activity station to compare your findings with other station participants.

Station #3: Texture Hunt

(blue owl nametag)

The outdoors is full of different textures. This touchy-feely hunt offers an opportunity to let your fingers do the walking to discover, identify, and classify a variety of textures.

Materials
Collecting bags
Paper
Pencils
8" x 8" pieces of poster board
Glue
Blindfolds
Two or three completed texture boards

What to Do
1. Each family chooses a collecting bag.
2. Take a walk around the backyard and gather textured objects, such as rocks, twigs, leaves, soil, or grass in the collecting bag.
3. As you collect objects, identify their source and record this information on paper.
4. Return to the blue activity station. Glue the collection onto a piece of poster board to make a texture board.
5. If desired, group objects into categories, such as rough, smooth, bumpy, hard, soft, slimy, and so on.
6. Write your family's name on the poster board and attach the identification list to the poster board. Allow to dry. If dry at the end of the meeting, take it home. If not, your child can bring it home when it is dry.

Station #4: Color Tally Cards

(green owl nametag)

The outdoors has many colors that are ever changing as seasons come and go. This activity develops an awareness of these colors and observation and recording skills.

Materials
Boxes of crayons
9" x 12" pieces of tagboard
Rulers

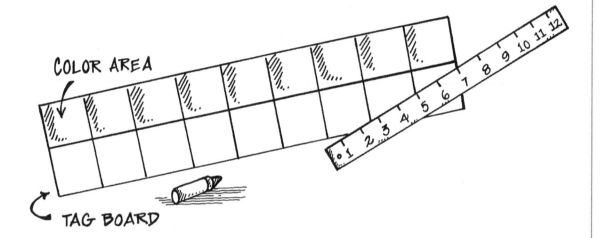

COLOR AREA

TAG BOARD

What to Do
1. Each family takes one piece of tagboard, a box of crayons, and a ruler.
2. Use the ruler to divide the tagboard into nine columns (see above).
3. Help your child use the crayons to color the top of each column with a different color. Leave one column blank for colors that do not match those represented. (Suggested colors are red, blue, green, purple, orange, yellow, brown, and black.)
4. Explore the outdoors. Each time you spot a color, let your child make a mark in the column under that color on the tally card.
5. When time is called, return to the green activity station and discuss and compare cards with other families. Did everyone find similar colors? Which color was found most often?

Thank everyone for coming and invite them to share a snack of seasonal fruit and crackers.

EVALUATION

Come and See Whoo's Outside

Family Meeting Evaluation

How did our workshop make you feel?

WIDE-AWAKE

DROWSY

OUT LIKE A LIGHT

ZZZZZZZZ

Comments and Suggestions

_____

_____

_____

_____

_____

_____

_____

Thank you for coming!

INVITATION

Cool Kids Cooking: A Make-It and Taste-It Workshop for Families

Easy!
Fun!
Tasty!
Nutritious!
Cool!
Safe!

We'll make practical step-by-step nutritional recipes that are fun, safe, and easy to prepare without HEAT!

Date _____
Time _____
Place _____

Who's Invited: The whole family

Dress for fun!

Please complete and detach the form below by _____ to reserve a space for your family.

- -

_____ Yes, we will attend the "Cool Kids Cooking" family meeting.
_____ Sorry, we will be unable to attend the meeting.

Child's name _____
Number of adults attending _____ Number of children attending _____

If you have questions or need transportation, please call _____.

Name _____ Phone _____
Email address _____

REMINDER

Taste-It Family Workshop."

Date _____

Time _____

Place _____

Who's Invited: The whole family

Dress comfortably and come prepared to have fun! Your family will be making and tasting some terrific recipes. We guarantee that the cooking will be cool as all recipes will be prepared without heat.

If you haven't made your reservation, please call _____ no later than _____.

Content Areas
Language
Literacy
Math
Motor Skills
Problem Solving/Critical Thinking
Social-Emotional Development

Purpose
To provide families with practical, step-by-step, nutritional recipes that are fun, safe, and easy to prepare without heat.

Note: Be aware of food allergies children may have. Some of the more common foods to which children may be allergic are wheat, milk and milk products, juices that have a high acid content such as orange or grapefruit, chocolate, eggs, and nuts. When families call to make reservations, tell them the foods that will be used at this meeting. Cultural and ethnic customs also influence the food families eat; some may have restricted dietary patterns and food preferences. A family's cultural heritage often determines whether a particular food will be eaten, regardless of its nutritional value. Talk with families about their food preferences and restrictions, and modify the food, as necessary.

Related Book
Pretend Soup and Other Real Recipes by Mollie Katzen and Ann Henderson

Nametags

Materials
Red, yellow, white, and brown construction paper
Masking tape
Pencils
Patterns of items on the food pyramid (see next page)
Markers

- Make nametags using the food patterns (see below). Make each shape in a different color, such as red apples, yellow cashew nut, brown bread, and white milk.
- Assign one food to each family.
- Different food nametags will be used to assign families to one of four activity stations.
- Make an extra set of nametags of each of the four foods to post at the activity stations.

© Gryphon House, Inc. 800.638.0928 www.gryphonhouse.com
Publisher permits photocopying of this page for distribution

Mixer—Pyramid Food Guide Puzzles

- As families arrive, distribute the nametags.
- Ask each family member to write his or her name on a nametag and use masking tape to attach it to his or her clothing.
- Be sure all members of each family have the same type of nametag so they can work together at each activity station.
- Enlarge the nametag patterns and trace them onto poster board.
- Cut each pattern into several puzzle pieces. Mix the pieces together in a basket or cardboard box.
- Pass the basket around the room and ask each family to take one puzzle piece. (Make sure there are enough puzzle pieces so all families can participate.)
- Say, "Each family has a puzzle piece of a food item from the Food Guide Pyramid. Please find other families that have matching colored puzzle pieces, introduce yourselves, and fit the puzzle pieces together."

Distribute copies of the *Food Guide Pyramid: A Guide of Daily Food Choices. The Food Guide Pyramid for Young Children* is in the public domain so written permission is not required to duplicate it. The website is http://www.usda.gov. Search for Food Guide Pyramid for Kids. Copies of the pyramid may also be distributed. Additional websites are provided below.

Food Guide Pyramid for Kids—The United States Department of Agriculture's guide assists families in choosing nutritious foods. http://www.oregonstate.edu. Search for Food Guide Pyramid for Kids.

Ethnic/Cultural and Special Audience Food Guide Pyramid—Provides Bilingual Food Guide Pyramids in 30 languages. http://www.nalusda.gov/fnic/etext/000023

Kids Food Cyber Club—Fun food facts, games and quizzes to learn which foods are good for growing bodies. http://www.kidfood.org/kf_cyber.html

Introduction

The preschool years are an excellent time to present the simple basic principles of good nutrition and how they relate to the health and well being of children. Nutrition education also relates to many curricular areas, including:

Social Emotional Development—Children learn to work together in both small and large groups, gain self-confidence as they master food preparation skills, and broaden their sense of cultures as they prepare and taste ethnic foods.

Language Development and Pre-Literacy Skills—Children read picture recipes, use food names and names of utensils used in food preparation, and communicate with parents, teachers, and peers as they eat prepared items.

Cognitive Development—Children measure and count recipe ingredients.

Science Concepts—Children combine and prepare foods. Children learn to follow directions as they add various ingredients.

Motor Development—Children develop hand and finger dexterity as they cut, measure, mix, serve, and eat foods.

What we eat and with whom we eat is influenced by our families. Adult and peer group eating habits are powerful models that establish children's decisions about their own food choices.

The four food activity stations show that food preparation can be done without the worry of hot stoves or boiling water. Each station has a "cool" treat. The station where each family begins is designated by their nametag pattern. The activity stations are:

1. Fruit Kabobs (red apple)
2. Pudding Shakes (white milk)
3. Traffic Light Crackers (brown bread)
4. Rice Cake Faces (yellow cashew)

After about 15 minutes a bell will ring, signalling families to move clockwise from the first activity station to the next.

Safety Considerations: Ask families to let you know if they have a food allergy to any of the foods that you will prepare and eat at this workshop.

Note: Ask participants to wash and dry their hands prior to starting each station. Make dry wipes available if there is no easily accessible water source.

COOL KIDS COOKING

75

Station #1—Fruit Kabobs (red apple nametags)

Materials

Toothpicks
Bananas, apples, oranges, or other fruit
Paper plates and bowls
Cutting boards
Knives, plastic or sharp (adults only)

What to Do

1. Help your child cut banana wheels (¼" thick) and slice apples and oranges into small wedges.
2. Place in paper bowls.
3. Help your child alternate one different piece of fruit on the toothpick to complete the fruit kabob.
4. Eat!

Station #2—Pudding Shakes

(white milk nametag)

Materials

Instant pudding (variety of flavors)
Milk
Clean, sterilized baby food jars with lids
Teaspoon measuring spoons
Measuring cups
Spoons for all participants
Tape or CD of "Shake Your Booty" by KC and the Sunshine Band or "Alice's Restaurant" by Arlo Guthrie (optional)

What to Do

1. Help your child measure 3 teaspoons of dry instant pudding mix into individual baby food jars.
2. Let them taste the dry powder. Can they recognize the flavor?
3. Add ⅓ cup of milk into each jar.
4. Secure the lid on the jar.
5. Shake. Count as you shake the jars to the beat of the song "Shake Your Booty" or "Alice's Restaurant."
6. Watch how the powder dissolves and the liquid thickens.
7. After the liquid thickens, let it set for a few minutes. Use this time to tidy up the station.
8. Now you have pudding! Remove the lid and eat.

Station #3—Traffic Light Crackers

(brown bread nametag)

Materials

Crackers

Peanut butter

Red, yellow, and green M & M's (healthier alternatives are cherry tomatoes, green grapes, and small pineapple chunks. Candy, although not considered a food group, is at the top of the food pyramid, so limit your servings.)

Plastic knives

Napkins

What to Do

1. Spread peanut butter on the crackers.
2. Put red, yellow, and green candies on the cracker, or place the fruits on the crackers.
3. Talk about the colors and what they mean when you cross the street or are riding in a car or on a bus.
4. Eat!

Station #4—Rice Cake Faces

(yellow cashew nut nametag)

Materials

Rice cakes or crackers

Peanut butter

Raisins

Knives

Napkins

What to Do

(Two tablespoons of peanut butter counts as one ounce of lean meat.)

1. Spread peanut butter on the rice cake.
2. Put raisins on the peanut butter to make a face.
3. Eat!

EVALUATION

Cool Kids Cooking

Family Meeting Evaluation

How cool was the workshop?

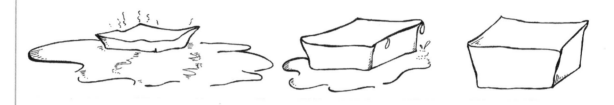

Not cool.   Kind of cool.   Really cool!

Comments and Suggestions

_____

_____

_____

_____

_____

_____

_____

_____

Thank you for coming!

INVITATION

Discovering Our Unique Qualities

Calling all super sleuths!

We would like to invite you and your family to an evening devoted to self-discovery.

As children (and adults!) learn more about themselves, they learn how to address everyday situations more effectively. We have planned an evening of activities to help us see what makes each of us special and how we can increase self-esteem.

We hope you can join the fun as we search for clues to help us discover who we are.

Date _____
Time _____
Place _____

Who's Invited: The whole family

Dress casually.

Refreshments will be served.

Please complete and detach the form below by _____ to reserve a space for your family.

- -

_____ Yes, we will attend the "Discovering Our Unique Qualities" family meeting.
_____ Sorry, we are unable to attend the meeting.

Child's name _____
Number of adults attending _____ Number of children attending _____

If you have questions or need transportation, please call _____.

Name _____ Phone _____
Email address _____

REMINDER

Discovering Our Unique Qualities

Just a reminder...

We'll be looking for you at our family meeting!

There is still time to register for our family meeting, which will address self-concept and self-esteem. Please call _____ as soon as possible so we can add your name to our list of super sleuths!

Snacks will be served.

Dress casually.

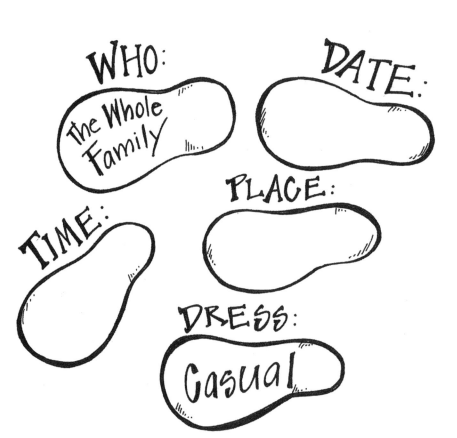

WHO: the Whole Family

DATE:

TIME:

PLACE:

DRESS: Casual

Content Areas

Art
Literacy
Math
Social Development

Purpose

To foster positive self-esteem in the development of young children, to foster competence based on their strengths, and to help children get along better with others.

Related Books

The Carrot Seed by Ruth Krauss
The Little House by Virginia Lee Burton
Mike Mulligan and His Steam Shovel by Virginia Lee Burton
Stand Tall, Molly Lou Melon by Patty Lovell
The Story of Ferdinand by Munro Leaf

Nametags

Materials

Red, yellow, green, and orange construction paper
Masking tape
Pencils
Patterns (see next page)
Markers

- Use the patterns (see next page) to make nametags. Make each shape a different color, such as a red magnifying glass, a yellow footprint, a green fingerprint, and an orange hound dog.
- Assign one pattern per family.
- Use the nametags to assign families to one of four activity stations.
- Make an extra set of nametags in each of the four patterns to post at the activity stations.

Mixer

- As families arrive, distribute the nametags.
- Ask each family member to write his or her name on the nametag and use masking tape to attach it to his or her clothing.
- Be sure that all members of each family have the same color nametag so they will work together at each activity station.
- Distribute Clue Worksheets (see page 88) to families as they put their nametags on. Explain that they will be detectives as they try to find people who fit the description on their worksheets.
- Allow approximately five minutes for this activity.

Introduction

The activities in this family meeting will help children learn about their individuality. They will see how they are similar to and different from other family members and friends. As children become more aware of their uniqueness, they will appreciate others for their individuality.

Share what families discovered from the Clue Worksheets. Ask who met someone new or who was able to complete the entire sheet. Explain that the nametags designate at which station families begin. If they have a nametag in the shape of a magnifying glass, they will begin at Station 1, which is designated by a magnifying glass. Those with a fingerprint nametag will begin at Station 2, designated by a fingerprint. Station 3 is designated by a hound, and Station 4 is designated by a footprint for those with a footprint nametag. Explain that the rotation will move clockwise. A signal, such as a bell or music, will inform families that they have approximately two to three minutes until it is time to rotate clockwise to the next station. The four activity stations are:

1. Take a Closer Look (magnifying glass)
2. "Thumb"thing's Going on Here! (fingerprint)
3. A Book About Me (hound)
4. I Am Special (footprint)

Station #1: Take a Closer Look

(magnifying glass nametag)

While genetics may be a difficult concept, children can have fun discovering similar and different traits among family members. The list (page 89) shows which traits are dominant (most likely to appear) and which are recessive (less likely to appear).

Materials
Mirrors
Lined paper
Dominant/Recessive Traits List (page 89)
Pencils

What to Do

1. Take a copy of the sheet listing dominant and recessive traits.
2. Go through the list, studying each family member to see which traits are present. Complete the form by putting each family member's name in the appropriate column. Use a mirror to check your traits.
3. After you have completed the form, share your discoveries with others at the station.

Station #2: "Thumb"thing's Going on Here!

(fingerprint nametag)

Look closely at thumbprints and then use them to create pictures.

Materials

Washable inkpads
Paper
Hand lenses or magnifying glasses
Washable markers
Tub of soapy water for washing hands
Paper towels

What to Do

1. Place your thumb on the inkpad. Make your thumbprint by gently pressing your thumb onto a piece of paper.
2. Use a hand lens or magnifying glass to study your thumbprint and the prints made by your family. Are they the same size? Who has the largest fingerprint in your family? Are they similar?
3. Make your thumbprint into an animal by adding legs, ears, and/or tails.
4. Make additional thumb and fingerprints. Add details with markers to create a picture.
5. Wash your hands and clean up your work area. Thank you!

Station #3: A Book About Me

(hound nametag)

Create unique books filled with illustrations and descriptions.

Materials

"All About Me" booklets (prepared prior to meeting)
Pencils
Crayons
Washable markers

What to Do

8 1/2" x 11" paper

Staplers

Booklets should consist of approximately eight pages.

1. Prior to the meeting, make an eight-page booklet (one for each family) by folding four 8 ½" x 11" pieces of paper and stapling them together

2. Choose eight of the following suggestions. Put one sentence at the top of each page. (Adjust the number of pages and the information on each page if necessary.)

Hi! My name is _____.

Something I am good at is _____.

I am _____ years old.

This is my home.

This is my family.

This is my pet.

I'm happy when...

I'm sad when...

I like to play _____.

My favorite food is _____.

My favorite color is _____.

My favorite book is _____.

3. At the meeting, each family takes an "All About Me" booklet.

4. Help the children complete the booklets, and encourage them to include some of their own ideas, if possible. If necessary, your child can dictate what to put on each page and then illustrate the ideas.

5. Share booklets with others at the station.

DISCOVERING OUR UNIQUE QUALITIES

Station #4: I Am Special

(footprint nametag)

Children will gain an understanding of individuality as they listen to *Leo the Late Bloomer* by Robert Kraus. They will learn that everybody does not develop at the same pace, and they will increase their self-esteem by realizing differences.

Materials
Leo the Late Bloomer by Robert Kraus
Clay

What to Do
1. One person in the group reads *Leo the Late Bloomer*.
2. As a group, discuss how Leo felt throughout the story. Ask the children how they would feel if they were Leo.
3. Talk about how Leo's parents felt. The parents can say how they would feel if they were Leo's parents.
4. Each person shares something they do well and how they feel when they do something well. Talk about why it is important to keep trying if you aren't successful at first.
5. Using the clay, each person makes a figure from the clay of something they do well.
6. Share something about your creation with the group.

Thank families for coming. Ask families to fill out an evaluation sheet and invite them to share a snack.

EVALUATION

Discovering Our Unique Qualities

Family Meeting Evaluation

We'd like to know what you thought about our meeting. Please give us a "clue" as to how we did.

Comments and Suggestions

_____

_____

_____

_____

_____

_____

_____

Thank you for coming!

WORKSHEET

Clue Worksheet

Clue #1: Find someone who
has curly hair. _____

Clue #2: Find someone whose name
begins with the letter A. _____

Clue #3: Find someone who is wearing
tennis shoes. _____

Clue #4: Find someone who works in a store. _____

Clue #5: Find someone who has blue eyes. _____

Clue #6: Find someone who has a brother. _____

Clue #7: Find someone who is left-handed. _____

Clue #8: Find someone who is new to
the community. _____

Clue #9: Find someone who is
chewing gum. _____

Clue #10: Find someone whose first
and last name start with the
same letter. _____

Clue #11: Find someone who likes to dance. _____

Clue #12: Find someone who ate a
sandwich today. _____

Clue #13: Find someone who is
wearing glasses. _____

Clue #14: Find someone who can snap
his or her fingers. _____

Clue #15: Find someone who owns a cat. _____

Dominant/Recessive Traits

Widow's Peak—V-shaped hairline on front of forehead	Present (dominant):	Not Present (recessive):
Dimples—They may be found on only one cheek or both. There may be more than one dimple on a cheek.	Present (dominant):	Not Present (recessive):
Tongue Rolling—Can you roll your tongue?	Can roll tongue (dominant):	Cannot roll tongue (recessive):
Thumb Position—Fold your hands so your fingers are interlocked. Which thumb is on top?	Left thumb on top (dominant):	Right thumb on top (recessive):
Eye Color—What color are your eyes? If your eyes are something other than blue or brown, please write the color next to your name.	Brown (dominant):	Blue (recessive):
Earlobes—Do your earlobes loop down (free) or are they attached?	Free (dominant):	Attached (recessive):

Dominant - Most likely to appear.   Recessive - Less likely to appear.

© Gryphon House, Inc. 800.638.0928 www.gryphonhouse.com
Publisher permits photocopying of this page for distribution

INVITATION

Exploring Our Community

Dear Parents,

We invite you to an evening of fun as we visit our greenhouse, post office, grocery store, and other community locations we have created in our classroom. Come ready to "work" to keep our businesses running successfully!

Date _____

Time _____

Place _____

Who's invited? The whole family

Remember to wear casual clothing for an evening of community fun.

Please join us after the activities for a special treat at our Classroom Ice Cream Shop!

Please detach and return by _____ or call _____ to reserve a place for your family.

_____Yes, we will attend the "Exploring Our Community" family meeting.
_____ No, we will not be able to attend.

Child's name _____

Number of adults attending _____ Number of children attending _____

If you have questions or need transportation, please call _____.

Name _____

Phone _____

Email address _____

Exploring Our Community

Just a reminder!

We look forward to seeing you at our family meeting on communities!

Date _____
Time _____
Place _____

Who's invited? The whole family

Don't forget to come dressed (casually) for an evening of community adventures!

A special treat will be provided at the end of our meeting.

If you haven't had a chance to RSVP, we still have room for more. Please call _____ to reserve your spot in our community.

Content
Dramatic Play
Math
Problem Solving
Social Development
Social Studies (Community)

Purpose
To discover the value of communities and the people who work and live there and to learn about various occupations and the tools and equipment used by the workers through various games and hands-on activities.

Related Books
Career Day by Anne Rockwell
Firefighters A to Z by Chris L. Demarest
Night Shift Daddy by Eileen Spinelli

Nametags

Materials
Red, yellow, green, and orange construction paper
Patterns of a plant, a question mark, a map, and a graduation cap (see next page)
Markers
Scissors

- Use the patterns (see next page) to make nametags. Use one color for each pattern, such as a red book, a green plant, and so on.
- Assign one shape per family.
- The different colored nametags will be used to assign families to one of four activity stations.
- Make an extra set of nametags in each of the four shapes to post at the activity stations.

NAME:

NAME:

NAME

NAME:

EXPLORING OUR COMMUNITY

Mixer

- As families arrive, distribute the nametags.
- Ask family members to write their names on the nametags and use masking tape to attach it to their clothing.
- Be sure all members of each family have the same color nametag so they will work together at each activity station.
- Make a grid card with different occupations written on each square, such as letter carrier, banker, plumber, or nurse. (Check the occupations of the participants ahead of time so you can be sure to have their jobs listed on the cards.) Give one to each family.
- The object of the mixer is for players to find people who perform the jobs on their cards. They must find people within a five-minute time frame. When they find a person whose job is listed on the card, they write that person's name in the appropriate square. After five minutes, ask everyone to regroup in a central meeting area.

Introduction

There are many people and businesses in a community. Without these people and the services they provide, our lives would be a lot harder. It is important for children to learn about their community. The activities in this family meeting will help children learn about some of the different types of businesses that help make up a community. They will see that it is important for everyone to work together in order for a community to be successful. Invite parents to give a brief description of their jobs.

Tell the group to watch and listen for a signal (lights flicked off and on, bell, whistle, or the song "Who Are the People in Your Neighborhood?"). When they hear that signal, they have two to three minutes before it is time to move clockwise to the next center. The activity station at which families begin corresponds to their nametags. The activity centers are:

1. Job Concentration (graduation cap)
2. Let's Get Growin' (plant)
3. Guess Who I Am! (question mark)
4. Mapping Activity (map)

Family Meeting Activities

Station #1: Job Concentration

(graduation cap nametag)

Learn about community workers and the services they provide. Vary this to meet the developmental stage of the children. The number of cards can be increased or decreased, or all the cards can be shuffled together instead of keeping the two sets separate.

Materials

12 index cards with drawings or magazine pictures of community workers, such as a police officer, doctor, librarian, or plumber

12 index cards with drawings or magazine pictures showing the community workers at work, such as a librarian checking books out or a plumber working under a sink

What to Do

1. Keep the two sets of cards separate. Shuffle the first set and place it face down in two columns with six cards in each column.
2. Shuffle the second set of cards and place them face down in two columns next to the first set of cards.
3. Take turns flipping the cards over, trying to match the workers with they jobs they perform.
4. If the cards match, keep the pair. If not, flip the cards over so they are face down.
5. Continue the game until all the cards have been matched and removed from the table.
6. The player with the most cards wins.

Station #2: Let's Get Growin'

(plant nametag)

Explore working in a greenhouse and doing a scientific experiment to see how seeds grow in different kinds of soil.

Materials

Newspapers

Craft sticks

Containers such as plastic cups, milk cartons, or small clay pots

Seeds (radish or marigold germinate and grow quickly)

Potting soil or other nutrient-rich soil

Poor quality soil (preferably clay or sandy soil)
A container for watering the newly planted seeds
Water, soap, and paper towels for cleanup
Permanent markers (adults only)

What to Do
During this activity, stress working and cleaning up together so the children learn the importance of shared responsibility.

1. Begin by covering the work surface with newspaper for quick and easy cleanup.
2. Each family takes two containers and two craft sticks. Write your name on your containers using a permanent marker (adults only). Also write "Potting Soil" on one craft stick and "Clay Soil" or "Sandy Soil" (depending on what type of soil is used) on the other craft stick.
3. Help your child fill one container with potting soil and the other with clay or sandy soil. Place the craft stick with the appropriate label in the soil-filled containers.
4. Take six seeds. Plant three seeds in each container according to directions on the packet.
5. After planting the seeds, help your child water their "soon-to-be" plants.
6. Help your child place the container in a location in the room where it will not be disturbed. (The plants will stay at the center or school so the children can observe their growth over the next few weeks.)
7. Clean the work areas by rolling up the newspaper and placing it in the trash. Wash your hands in the pan of soapy water and dry with the paper towels.

Station #3: Guess Who I Am!

(question mark nametag)

Learn about the tools used in a variety of professions while playing this game where players guess occupations when tools from different trades are displayed.

Materials
Assortment of tools that people in different occupations use. Below is a list of possible items and the professionals who use them. This list can be modified to reflect the occupations found in your community.

- Stethoscope, white jacket—Doctor
- Blueprints, ruler—Architect
- Plunger, wrench—Plumber
- Hammer, building square, levels—Carpenter
- Paintbrush, can of paint—Painter
- Thermometer, clipboard—Nurse

- Pretend money, deposit bag—Banker
- Chef's hat, cooking utensils—Chef/cook
- Pencils, message pad, telephone—Receptionist
- Apron, mixing bowl, spatula—Baker
- Flowers, pruning shears—Florist

8 ½" x 6 ½" pieces of paper
Pencils

What to Do
1. Begin by talking about how all workers have special tools or items that they use in their daily work.
2. Each family takes a few pieces of 8 ½" x 6 ½" paper and a pencil.
3. The group selects one person. That person picks one profession, holds up a tool (such as the stethoscope), and then asks the group what professional or worker uses this tool while they work.
4. After a short family discussion, one member from each family writes down their guess.
5. Display all of the guesses to see which families have the correct answer.
6. If no one guesses the correct occupation, display another tool from the same occupation.
7. If no one guesses the correct answer after all tools are displayed, identify which occupation the tools are used for.
8. If any time remains, one person can mime what he or she does as an occupation and the group can try to guess the occupation!

Station #4: Mapping Activity

(map nametag)

Make a map to share with other members of the group at the activity station.

Materials
12 x 16" white construction paper
9 ½" x 11" graph paper
Pencils, crayons, or colored pencils
Erasers
Rulers
Sample maps of houses and backyards

What to Do
1. As a family, draw a map of your apartment, home, or backyard.
2. Use plain white paper or graph paper and pencils, crayons, or colored pencils to draw your maps.

3. After 10 minutes, share your maps with the other people at the station.
4. After sharing all the maps, look for things in common among maps, such as number of rooms, number of bedrooms, swing set, family room, and so on.

Group Activity—A Visit to the Ice Cream Shop

Once all activities are complete, invite the group to come to the "Ice Cream Shop" where they will make Baggie Ice Cream. Beforehand, set up an assembly line with ingredients for the ice cream. Display a poster-size picture recipe for everyone to see and follow (see illustration on next page). Depending on the size of the meeting, two assembly lines may be necessary to expedite this activity. Each bag will make enough ice cream for four to five people so form groups accordingly. Encourage children to measure and add the ingredients to the bag. An adult will need to seal and tape the bags closed.

Baggie Ice Cream

Each group of four or five will need the following materials:

$1/4$ cup sugar
1 cup milk
1 cup whipping cream or half-and-half
$1/2$ teaspoon vanilla extract
1 cup rock salt
Ice

$3/4$ cup water
1 gallon zipper-closure freezer bag
1 quart zipper-closure freezer bag
Duct tape
Plastic spoons
8 oz. cups to hold ice cream
Towels

Recipe

1. Place 1 cup milk in the quart bag, add 1 cup whipping cream, and then add $1/4$ cup sugar. Finally, add $1/2$ teaspoon of vanilla extract.
2. Seal the bag tightly. Use duct tape to secure the seal on the zipper end of the baggie.
3. Place the baggie with the ice cream ingredients inside the gallon baggie.
4. Pack ice into the gallon baggie, placing it around the small bag. Add rock salt and $3/4$ cup of water. Seal this bag tightly. Use duct tape to seal the gallon baggie.
5. Each group of four or five forms a small circle. Wrap towels around the gallon-size baggie to protect hands from the cold. (Mittens can also be used!) Take turns shaking the bag until the ingredients are frozen (about 10-15 minutes).

6. Once the ice cream is frozen, the gallon-size bag should be opened and thrown away. Open the quart bag and serve the ice cream by scooping it into the cups for the participants. Provide toppings, if desired.

Note: Anyone allergic to milk or milk products should not eat the ice cream. If this situation should arise, provide an alternative snack.

Baggie Ice Cream

large
small

Mix the following ingredients in the small baggie:

1 CUP OF MILK   1 CUP OF WHIPPING CREAM   ¼ CUP OF SUGAR   ½ TEASPOON VANILLA EXTRACT

 Seal the baggie with duct tape.

Place the small baggie inside the large baggie.

Add:

1 CUP OF ROCK SALT   ICE   ¾ CUPS WATER

Seal the large baggie with duct tape.

Shake until the ice cream ingredients are frozen.

Divide into small cups →

ENJOY!

© Gryphon House, Inc. 800.638.0928 www.gryphonhouse.com
Publisher permits photocopying of this page for distribution

Exploring Our Community

Family Meeting Evaluation

We hope you enjoyed your evening with us. Please share your thoughts on tonight's activities to help us prepare for future meetings. Circle the ice cream cone that shows how you felt about the meeting. Your comments are greatly appreciated!

The meeting was great!

The meeting was okay.

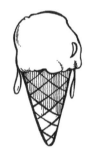

The meeting was not so good.

Comments and Suggestions

_____

_____

_____

_____

_____

Thank you for coming!

Exploring Our Senses

Are you ready for a fun-filled time?

Come with us as we explore the world of Chris van Allsburg's *Two Bad Ants*.

We will use our senses to explore the world around us. We will end our meeting with a picnic lunch. You won't want to miss the fun, so pack up the family for some exploring.

Date _____
Time _____
Place _____

Who's Invited: The whole family

Dress comfortably.

We will have a small picnic after our activities. Please bring a blanket and small snack. If the weather permits, we will have our picnic outside. Cookies will be provided.

Please detach and return by _____ or call _____ to reserve a place for your family.

- -

_____Yes, we'll come to the "Exploring Our Senses" family meeting.
_____ No, we can't attend.

Child's name _____
Number of adults attending _____ Number of children attending _____

If you have any questions or need transportation, please call _____.

Name _____ Phone_____
Email address _____

Exploring Our Senses

Don't forget!

The "Exploring Our Senses" family meeting is just around the corner!

We will be exploring our senses at _____ on from _____ to _____ .

Please dress comfortably and bring the family for lots of fun!

Please bring a small snack. We will provide cookies for dessert.

Please call _____ to RSVP as soon as possible if you have not responded yet. We always have room for more!

Content Areas

Art
Literacy
Math
Music and Movement
Problem Solving

Purpose

To use Chris Van Allsburg's humorous story, *Two Bad Ants,* to explore the world through the five senses.

Related Books

Mabela the Clever by Margaret Read MacDonald
My Five Senses by Aliki

Nametags

Materials

Ant pattern (see below)
Scissors
Pencils and markers
Copies of Ant Scavenger Hunt handout, one per person (see page 110)
Red, yellow, tan, gray, and brown construction paper
Masking tape

- Use the ant pattern (at right) to cut out nametags.
- Assign one color per family.
- Different colored nametags will be used to assign families to one of five activity stations.
- Make an extra set of nametags in each of the five colors to post at the activity stations.

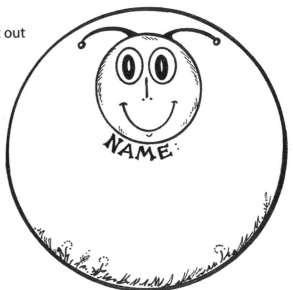

EXPLORING OUR SENSES

Mixer—Ant Scavenger Hunt

- As families arrive, distribute the nametags.
- Ask each family member to write his or her name on the nametag and use masking tape to attach it to his or her clothing.
- Be sure all members of each family have the same color nametag so they will work together at each activity station.
- Give each family a copy of the Ant Scavenger Hunt handout and a pencil (see page 110).
- Ask them to find people who have experienced an ant encounter that is on the list, and then write the person's name next to the "ant" encounter.

Introduction

After 5-10 minutes, reassemble the group. Read *Two Bad Ants* by Chris Van Allsburg. Discuss the importance of our five senses and briefly explain the stations. Explain that the color of the nametags corresponds to each family's first activity station. Inform families that you will turn the lights off and on *(demonstrate by turning the lights off and on)* two minutes before they are to rotate to the next station. The second time you turn the lights off and on, families should move clockwise to the next station. Ask families to go to the activity station designated by the color of their nametag to begin the activities. The five activity stations are:

1. The Nose Knows (red ant)
2. The Ants Go Marching On… (yellow ant)
3. Some Like It Hot, Some Like It Cold (tan ant)
4. Do You Feel What I Feel? (gray ant)
5. Crafty Ants (brown ant)

Family Meeting Activities

Station #1: The Nose Knows (sense of smell)

(red ant nametag)

Determine the accuracy of the sense of smell by using it to guess a variety of "mystery" smells.

Materials

8 items with strong scents, such as an orange cut in half, a bar of soap, cinnamon sticks, a cotton ball saturated in vanilla extract, coffee beans, a chocolate candy bar, a lemon cut in half, or a cotton ball saturated in peppermint extract
8 boxes with a small hole cut in one end of each
Copies of the Mystery Smell Worksheet (see page 111)
Pencils

What to Do

Before the family meeting, place each of the eight scented items in separate boxes, one item per box. Replace the lid so the items are hidden. Use masking tape and a marker to number the boxes from 1-8. Arrange the boxes so the end with the small hole faces the participants.

1. Smell through the small hole at the end of the box.
2. Write down what you think might be in the box on the Mystery Smell Worksheet.
3. After everyone has smelled the boxes and written down their guesses, remove the lids to reveal the items in the boxes.

Station #2: The Ants Go Marching On… (sense of sight and hearing)

(yellow ant nametag)

Everyone—yes, adults too!—will have an opportunity to see things from an ant's point of view, and then to draw a picture from an ant's point of view.

Materials

Paper
Crayons
Tape player
Cassette tape of *The Ants Go Marching On* or Joe Scrugg's *Ants*
Picture of an ant (large enough to show its special characteristics)

What to Do

1. As a group, talk about the characteristics of ants. Discuss their color, the number of legs they have (6), their size, and their antennas.
2. What do you think it would be like to be as small as an ant? What could you do and where could you go if you were the size of an ant?
3. Move about the area like ants. One person from the group plays music to let the others know when to begin moving. When the music stops, stop and look around to see the view. Play the music again. Repeat this process two or three times.
4. After finishing the group "ant crawl," talk about the things you saw.
5. Draw a picture from an ant's point of view. It can be a picture of something you saw on the ant crawl, or it can be a scene of your choice.

Station #3: Some Like It Hot, Some Like It Cold (sense of taste)

(tan ant nametag)

What's your preference? A warm mug of hot chocolate or a tall, cold glass of chocolate milk? Record responses to this and other "hot/cold" favorites on a graph while focusing on taste.

Materials
Copies of the graph for recording responses (see page 112)
Markers
Warm hot chocolate and cold chocolate milk
Small paper cups
Samples of other warm and cold foods and beverages such as carrots, applesauce, pizza, soft pretzels, and baked beans (use pictures of the foods and beverages or actual samples)

What to Do
1. Each person takes a copy of the graph.
2. Taste the warm hot chocolate and then taste the cold chocolate milk.
3. Which one did you like best? Mark your choice on the graph.
4. Repeat for each of the foods or beverages sampled.
5. After everyone has tasted the items and recorded their preference, use the graph to discuss the results.
Note: Check for any food allergies, especially to milk or chocolate.

Station #4: Do You Feel What I Feel? (sense of touch)

(gray ant nametag)

As the ants in the story marched on their mission to bring back more crystals, they crossed many different textures. Feel different items the ants walked on, as well as a variety of other objects, and sort them into various categories.

Materials
Small amount of soil
Blades of grass
Small rocks or pebbles
Pieces of smooth metal
Pieces of sandpaper
Pieces of felt
Pieces of cardboard
Coins
Sand

What to Do
1. Take a sample of each of the items listed above. Ask each member of your family to feel each object.
2. As you feel the objects, discuss how the object feels. Is it soft? Is it hard? Is it rough? Is it smooth?
3. Sort the items according to the texture of each object.
4. Share with other families what you found. Did everyone sort the objects into the same groups or did some have different results? Discuss how some objects can have more than one texture. For example, the felt could be considered both soft and smooth, or the rocks might be hard and smooth.
5. Put the items back as you found them so they are ready for the next group.

Station #5: Crafty Ants (sense of touch)

(brown ant nametag)

Develop fine motor skills while making "two bad ants" from pipe cleaners.

Materials
Black pipe cleaners
Several pairs of small wire cutters (adults only)
Example of a pipe cleaner ant
Picture of an ant

What to Do
(Display a picture of an ant that shows its features clearly, and display an example of a pipe cleaner ant.)
1. Using black pipe cleaners, work together as a family to make an ant. If the pipe cleaners need to be cut, carefully use the wire cutters to do so (adults only).
2. If time permits, play with your ants, perhaps performing a scene from *Two Bad Ants*.

Thank families for coming. Ask the families to fill out an evaluation form and stay for a picnic.

Exploring Our Senses

Family Meeting Evaluation

We want to know what you think!

Please take a minute to let us know about our meeting.

It was great!   It was okay.   It was not too good.

Please circle the ant that shows how you feel.

Comments and Suggestions

_____

_____

_____

_____

_____

_____

Thank you for coming!

Ant Scavenger Hunt

Below is a list of "Ant Encounters." Try to find people who have had the ant encounters listed on your sheet. When you find a person who has experienced the encounter, ask them to write their name on the appropriate line.

1. Someone who has had ants in their house in the past. _____

2. Someone who has ants in their house now. _____

3. Someone who has found ants in a picnic basket. _____

4. Someone who has been bitten by an ant. _____

5. Someone who owns an ant farm. _____

6. Someone who has had ants in their pants! _____

7. Someone who has seen a red ant. _____

8. Someone who has eaten an ant. _____

9. Someone who has watched ants build a nest. _____

10. Someone who has seen an ant carrying food. _____

11. Someone who owns a stuffed ant. _____

12. Someone who is afraid of ants. _____

13. Someone whose nickname is Ant. _____

14. Someone who likes to draw ants. _____

15. Someone whose initials are A.N.T. _____

16. Someone who has had an unusual ant event. _____

Mystery Smell Worksheet

1

2

3

4

5

6

7

8

Some Like It Hot, Some Like It Cold

Chocolate Milk		Carrots		Applesauce		Pizza		Baked Beans	
Hot	Cold	Hot	Cold	Hot	Cold	Hot	Cold	Hot	Cold

EXPLORING OUR SENSES

Family Book Worms!

INVITATION

Reading fun and activities for the whole family!

Enjoy literacy activities that promote a lifelong interest in reading.

Please Come!

Date:

Time:

Place:

Dress casually.

Refreshments will be served.

Please complete and detach the form below by _____ to reserve a space for your family.

_____ Yes, we will attend the "Family Bookworms" family meeting.
_____ Sorry, we are unable to attend the meeting.

Child's name _____
Number of adults attending _____ Number of children attending _____

If you have any questions or need transportation, please call _____

Name _____ Phone _____
Email address _____

Family Book Worms!

R E M I N D E R

Join us for reading fun for the whole family.

Please Come!

Date:

Time:

Place:

Who's Invited: The whole family

Dress for fun!

Refreshments will be served.

Call _____ and reserve a spot today. If you need transportation, let us know.

Content Areas

Art
Dramatic Play
Language
Literacy
Motor Skills

Purpose

To promote literacy awareness and provide families with literature and literacy activities to promote a lifelong interest in reading.

Nametags

Materials

Green, yellow, red, and orange construction paper
Black markers
Scissors
Bookworm nametag pattern (see below)

- Use the bookworm nametag pattern (see below) to make nametags in four colors.
- Assign one color per family.
- Different colored nametags will be used to assign families to one of four activity stations.
- Make an extra set of nametags in each of the four colors to post at the activity stations.

Mixer—Bookworm Hunt

- As families arrive, distribute the bookworm nametags.
- Ask each family member to write his or her name on the nametag and use masking tape to attach it to his or her clothing.
- Be sure all members of each family have the same color nametag so they can work together at each activity station.
- After families have arrived, give each family a copy of the "Find a Bookworm" Hunt (page 122).
- Ask them to move about the room and interact with other families while trying to complete their bookworm hunt.

Introduction

Reading aloud to children is one of the most significant parent/child activities that supports improved literacy. Reading aloud to children builds their understanding of concepts, develops oral language and vocabulary, promotes the joy and pleasure of reading, and develops a sense of the importance of literacy learning. There is a strong correlation between being read to at home and children's later success with reading.

Tell families they can proceed to the bookworm activity station that has the same color as their nametag. They will stay at that station until a bell rings as a signal to move clockwise to the next station. The activity stations are:

1. My Very Own Book (green bookworm)
2. The World of Print (yellow bookworm)
3. Let's Make a Puppet (red bookworm)
4. Time to Browse and Read to Your Child (orange bookworm)

Family Meeting Activities

Station #1: My Very Own Book
(green bookworm nametag)

Use inexpensive materials to make books that are easy to read.

Materials
8 ½" x 11" sheets of white paper
Colored yarn
Scissors
Crayons
Paper punch
Paste
Large variety of magazines with photos (collected
   from families prior to meeting)
Family photos

What to Do
1. Fold two sheets of paper in half.
2. Place folded sheets of paper together to
   make an eight-page booklet.
3. Make two holes in the fold of the sheets
   of paper with the paper punch.
4. Thread the yarn through the two holes
   and tie.
5. Ideas for book titles:

- Things I Like to Eat
- My Animal Book
- Things I Do Not Like
- Things I Like
- My Family

6. Write the title on the cover and let your child
   decorate it.
7. Help your child cut pictures from the magazines
   and place one or two pictures on each page.
8. Your child can also draw pictures and dictate
   captions.

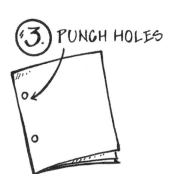

Station #2: The World of Print

(yellow bookworm nametag)

Learn about the many forms of print in the everyday environment, including signs, labels, logos, and symbols.

Materials

Examples of environmental print, such as store logos,
   cereal boxes, and so on
Poster board
Markers
Crayons
Scissors

What to Do

At this station, display a definition of environmental print: Print that is encountered outside of books and is a pervasive part of everyday living. Before this family meeting, draw a traffic light on poster board. Color each light with the appropriate markers. Write the word "stop" under the red light, "caution" under the yellow light, and "go" under the green light.

1. Show your child the poster board traffic light. Ask him or her what each of the lights signifies. If they do not know, explain what each color means.

2. Play "Red Light, Yellow Light, Green Light." Explain how traffic lights work and what the signals mean. Emphasize that the green light means "go" and the red light means "stop." Show the stoplight with the three words and colors.

3. Explain that when all the children in the group see the green light, they are to clap as fast as they can. When they see the yellow light, they should clap slowly, and when they see the red light, they should stop clapping.

4. One person uses his or her hands to cover up two lights, so only one light is visible.

5. Try this again with jumping, walking, or hopping.

6. Continue playing, which will help children associate the printed word "go" with the green light and the printed word "stop" with the red light.

7. Look at other everyday signs and logos and discover which ones the children can "read." For example, McDonald's, Hardee's, Target, Home Depot, Pizza, Pepsi, Coke, Dairy Queen, Kentucky Fried Chicken, Taco Bell, Subway, and so on.

Station #3: Let's Make a Puppet

(red bookworm nametag)

Make a puppet that can be used to reenact the motions of a story character as they listen to a favorite story.

Materials
Fabric scraps
Colored construction paper
Colored pipe cleaners
Crayons
Scissors
Yarn
Glue or stapler
Paper cylinders (toilet tissue or paper towel rolls)
Assortment of storybooks or books of nursery rhymes

What to Do
1. Glue or staple a piece of construction paper into a cylinder.
2. Decorate the paper cylinder with available materials.
3. Select a storybook or nursery rhyme that features a central character, such as *Where Can It Be?* by Ann Jones.
4. Encourage your child to act out the story with his or her puppets as you read the story or say the nursery rhyme.

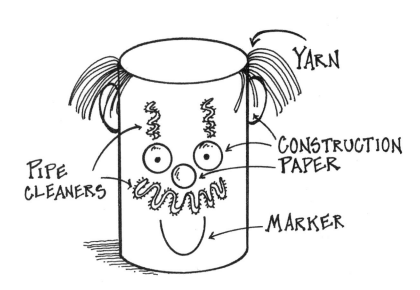

Station #4: Time to Browse and Read to Your Child

(orange bookworm nametag)

Share old tried-and-true children's storybook favorites as well as some of the newer books that appear to be destined to become future classics.

Materials

Children's books (about 3-5 per family)
Comfortable chairs on a large rug in the book corner
Handouts of suggested titles for children aged three through five years
  (see page 123)

What to Do

1. Take time to look at the books at this station. Many of the books may be familiar to you and your child and others may be new to you.
2. If possible, look at all of the books at this activity station. There may be time to browse further after the meeting.
3. Take a copy of the handouts that list recommended book titles and authors.

Thank everyone for coming and invite them to share a snack of seasonal fruit and crackers.

EVALUATION

Family Bookworms

Family Meeting Evaluation

We would like to know what you thought about the "Family Bookworms" meeting. Please circle the picture that best describes your feelings. We appreciate your feedback, so feel free to make comments. Thank you.

Good apple   So-so   Rotten apple

Comments and Suggestions

_____

_____

_____

_____

_____

_____

Thank you for coming!

"Find a Bookworm" Hunt

Collect a different person's signature (either child or adult) for each item on the mixer sheet.

Find someone who has read:

a story about a dog   _____

a book this week   _____

a book to their child(ren) this week   _____

Gone with the Wind   _____

Alice in Wonderland   _____

Peter Pan   _____

a book about crafts   _____

a book about Clifford, the big red dog   _____

a mystery   _____

a Harry Potter book   _____

a book about saving our environment   _____

a book about a horse   _____

a book of poetry   _____

a comic book   _____

a romance book   _____

a book on parenting   _____

a cookbook   _____

a book checked out from the
  public library   _____

a book purchased from a bookstore   _____

a book purchased on the Internet   _____

BOOK LIST

Abiyoyo by Pete Seeger

Alexander and the Terrible, Horrible, No Good, Very Bad Day by Judith Viorst

Bedtime for Frances by Russell Hoban

Blueberries for Sal by Robert McCloskey

Bread and Jam for Frances by Russell Hoban

Brown Bear, Brown Bear, What Do You See? by Bill Martin, Jr.

Can I Keep Him? by Steven Kellogg

The Cat in the Hat by Dr. Seuss

Changes, Changes by Pat Hutchins

Chicka Chicka Boom Boom by Bill Martin, Jr. and John Archambault

Chicken Little by Laura Rader

Chicken Little by Steven Kellogg

Corduroy by Don Freeman

The Doorbell Rang by Pat Hutchins

The First Snowfall by Anne and Harlow Rockwell

Flossie and the Fox by Patricia McKissack

Flying by Donald Crews

Frog on His Own by Mercer Mayer

Goldilocks and the Three Bears by Jan Brett

Green Eggs and Ham by Dr. Seuss

"The Green Grass Grew All Around" (many versions)

Hello Kangaroo by Nan Bodsworth

Henny Penny by Paul Galdone (illustrator)

I Don't Want to Go to School by Christine Harris

If You Give a Mouse a Cookie by Laura Joffe Numeroff

If You Give a Pig a Pancake by Laura Joffe Numeroff

Imogene's Antlers by David Small

Island of the Skog by Steven Kellogg

It's Pumpkin Time by Zoe Hall

Jamberry by Bruce Degen

The Judge by Margot and Harve Zemach

Just Like You and Me by David Miller

Koala Lou by Mem Fox

Leo the Late Bloomer by Robert Kraus

A Letter to Amy by Ezra Jack Keats

"The Little Red Hen" (many versions)

Look Book by Tana Hoban

Make Way for Ducklings by Robert McCloskey

The Mitten by Jan Brett

Mouse Paint by E.S. Walsh

The Napping House by Audrey and Don Wood

Over in the Meadow by Ezra Jack Keats

Owl Moon by Jane Yolen

Pancakes for Breakfast by Tomie DePaola

Picasso the Green Tree Frog by Amanda Graham

Rosie's Walk by Pat Hutchins

Silly Sally by Audrey Wood

The Snowy Day by Ezra Jack Keats

Swimmy by Leo Lionni

There Was an Old Lady by Simms Taback

"The Three Billy Goats Gruff"

Titch by Pat Hutchins

Tough Boris by Mem Fox

The Very Busy Spider by Eric Carle

The Very Hungry Caterpillar by Eric Carle

Wacky Wednesday by Theo Le Sieg

Whistle for Willie by Ezra Jack Keats

Zoom by Istvan Banyai

FAMILY BOOKWORMS!

Family Game Night

Dear family,
You are all invited to come to a night of fun as we explore the world of games. We value play as a way of learning, and by attending this fun-filled meeting you will see how we include it in our curriculum. The meeting will last for about an hour and a half. You and your children will have the opportunity to play some games. By the end of the meeting you will have an understanding of the importance of play in the lives of your children as they grow and develop. You will also learn about simple and inexpensive games that you and your child can make and play at home.

Please help us by bringing an assortment of buttons and some empty egg cartons, which will be used to make take-home games.

Please dress casually.

The meeting will be on _____. It will start at _____ and will end with refreshments being served.

If you are able to attend, please return the bottom portion of this letter by _____ or call _____and let us know how many will be attending.

____Yes, we'll come to the "Family Game Night" family meeting
____ No, we can't attend.

Number of adults attending _____ Number of children attending _____
We can bring buttons _____ We can bring egg cartons_____

If you have any questions or need transportation, please call _____.

Name _____ Phone _____
Email address _____

REMINDER

Family Game Night

Find your way to _____ for the "Family
Game Night" family meeting.

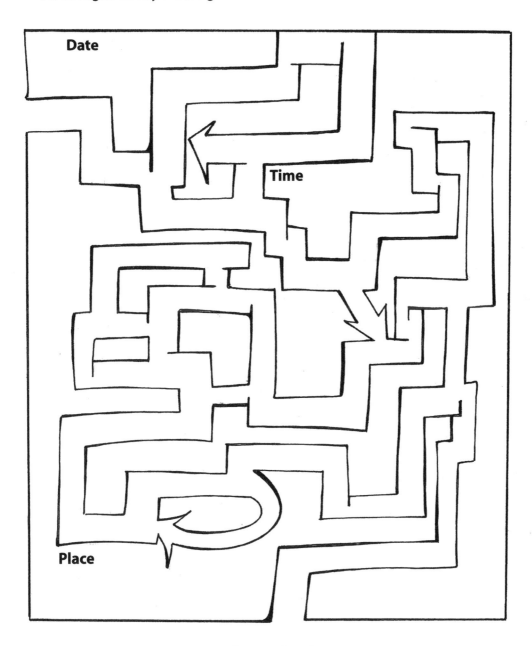

Come join us!

Content Areas
Math
Motor Skills
Problem Solving
Social Development

Purpose
To explore games as a means of enhancing children's social, cognitive, and motor skills.

Nametags

Materials
Red, yellow, green, and blue, and white construction paper
Scissors
Pattern (see next page)
Markers

Parents' Nametags

- Trace the nametag pattern (see next page) on red, yellow, green, blue, and white construction paper and cut out the blocks.
- Assign one color per family. The different colored nametags will be used to assign families to one of five activity stations.
- Make an extra set of nametags in each of the five colors to post at the activity stations.
- Write the name of this center or school in the top block.
- Leave the bottom left block blank so that the parent can write his or her name in it.
- In the bottom right block, write, "I'm _____'s playmate." The parents will write the name of their child in this space.

Children's Nametags

- Follow the directions for the parent nametag.
- The bottom left block will also be blank so the child can write his/her name in it.
- Place a gold star sticker in the bottom right block.

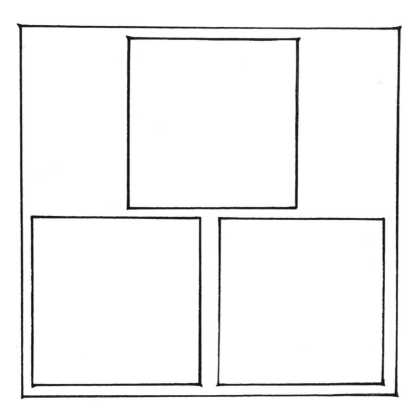

Mixer—Find Someone Who...

Materials
Mixer sheet (see page 133)
Pencils or crayons

- As families arrive, distribute the nametags.
- Ask each family member to write his or her name and use masking tape to attach it to his or her clothing.
- Be sure that all members of each family have the same color nametag so they will work together at each activity station.
- Distribute the mixer sheets (page 133) and pencils.
- Explain that you want the families to move around the room and to interact with one another while trying to find someone that will fit one of the descriptions on the sheet.
- Remind them to collect a different person's signature (either child or adult) for each item.

FAMILY GAME NIGHT

Introduction

The games at this family meeting require the participants to play together, rather than against each other. The emphasis will be on total participation spontaneity, sharing, playing our best, and recognizing that every player is important. While we are having fun, we will also be focusing on motor development. Three-year-olds, four-year-olds, and five-year-olds are beginning to control their small muscles while the large muscles are still growing. They are using these large muscles as they run, jump, climb, skip, hop, throw, and catch. The games in this family meeting use both small muscles (fine motor) and large muscles (gross motor). Games provide an excellent way for children to learn as they are having fun. When children play games they:

● learn about cooperation and teamwork, trust, and group unity.
● increase their vocabulary by learning to identify objects, pictures, and materials.
● develop their senses of sight, hearing, and touch.
● learn to discriminate and classify materials.
● learn to follow directions and to take turns.
● discover cause and effect.
● gain experience and social skills with other children and adults.

Families go to the activity station that is the same color as their nametag. They will rotate clockwise to the next station when they hear the whistle (or bell). The five activity stations are:

1. Beach Ball Buddy Balancing (red nametag)
2. Balloon Minton (blue nametag)
3. Put the Tail on the Donkey Helpers (yellow nametag)
4. Make-It-and-Take-It Shape Up Game (green nametag)
5. Make-It-and-Take-It Egg Carton Button Game (white nametag)

Family Meeting Activities

Station #1—Beach Ball Buddy Balancing

(red nametag)

Exercise large muscles.

Materials
Five or six medium-size beach balls or large rubber balls, depending on the number of participants (six participants will need three balls)

What to Do
1. Pair up with your child or with another member of the group.
2. Face your partner and balance the ball between your bodies without using your hands. (Hold your hands at your sides after you place the ball between your bodies.)
3. One partner calls out movements, such as "walk sideways", "walk forward" or "walk backward","turn in a complete circle," and so on.
4. Try this with more than one ball.
5. If your child has trouble keeping the ball from falling, let him or her hold it with his or her hands.

Station # 2: Balloon-Minton

(blue nametag)

Exercise and develop large muscles of the body and develop counting skills.

Materials
Large balloons
String or rope to serve as a net, or if available, a badminton net
Two chairs
Note: Have an extra supply of balloons in case there is a popping problem.

What to Do
1. Tie a string between two chairs to serve as a net.
2. Divide the families at the station into two groups.
3. One group goes to each side of the net.
4. Together, count the number of times you hit the balloon back and forth over the net.

Caution: Be sure to pick up and remove all balloons and pieces of balloons as they pose a choking hazard.

Station # 3: Put the Tail on the Donkey Helpers

(yellow nametag)

Practice large and fine motor skills.

Materials
Picture of a donkey
Donkey tail
Masking tape
Blindfold

What to Do
1. Blindfold one participant.
2. The rest of the group gives directions to the blindfolded person. The object is to get the donkey's tail taped onto the right place.
3. Shout out instructions, such as " Higher!" "Lower!" "No, the other way!"
4. Continue play until all participants have had a turn taping the tail to the donkey.

Station #4: Make-It-and-Take-It Shape Up Game

(green nametag)

Learn the names of shapes and exercise the large muscles of the body.

Materials
Poster board or construction paper
Markers
Scissors
Index cards
Masking tape
Patterns of the following shapes: circle, triangle, rectangle (large patterns for floor shapes and small patterns for index card shapes)

What to Do
1. Trace large patterns on poster board and cut out two of each shape.
2. Trace small pattern shapes on index cards, creating five index cards with circles, five with triangles, and five with rectangles.
3. Tape the completed large patterns to the floor.
4. Place index cards face down.

5. One child from the group draws a card, finds the matching shape, and then stands on it until all the cards have been drawn. If a shape is repeated, the child moves to the matching shape. Each family member can have a turn.

6. Repeat the game, instructing the players to hop (if able), walk backwards, or move in any other way to each shape.

7. You can also play a variation of this game using the numbers 1 through 10 or colors.

8. Take your game home.

Station #5: Make-It-and-Take-It Egg Carton Button Game

(white nametag)

Develop small motor skills by sorting buttons by shape, number, and color.

Materials

Empty egg cartons (one for each family)
Variety of buttons of different sizes and colors
Markers
Containers to hold buttons
Note: Ask families to bring an assortment of buttons to the meeting.

What to Do

(Prior to the family meeting, write numbers 0 through 10 or 1 through 5 in the egg carton compartments.)

1. Take one egg carton and an assortment of buttons.

2. Ask your child to count out the buttons and place the appropriate amount in each egg carton compartment.

3. Play a variation of this game by letting your child sort the buttons by shape and color.

Thank everyone for coming and invite them to share a snack of seasonal fruit and crackers.

EVALUATION

Family Game Night

Family Meeting Evaluation

Let us know how you felt about the "Family Game Night" family meeting by circling the clown face that describes your feelings.

Please circle one.

Great!   OK   Not so good.

Comments and Suggestions

_____

_____

_____

_____

Thank you for coming!

Family Game Night Mixer Sheet

Move around the room and interact with the other families, while trying to find someone that will fit one of the descriptions on the sheet. Collect a different person's signature (either child or adult) for each item.

1. Knows what colors the squares are on a checkerboard _____

2. Owns the game Chinese checkers _____

3. Can play chess _____

4. Has played the game Candyland _____

5. Works crossword puzzles _____

6. Has played connect the dots _____

7. Can describe how to play Go Fish _____

8. Has put together a puzzle in the last month _____

9. Has played Twister in the last five years _____

10. Knows how to play Solitaire _____

11. Plays dominoes _____

12. Has a Playstation at home _____

13. Can play Backgammon _____

14. Has an Etch-A-Sketch at home _____

15. Has played Charades in the last year _____

16. Has recently played Musical Chairs _____

17. Has ever made a game to play _____

© Gryphon House, Inc. 800.638.0928 www.gryphonhouse.com
Publisher permits photocopying of this page for distribution

FAMILY GAME NIGHT

Get Ready, Get Set, Move!

Come and help your child develop physical skills, including competency in body management and spatial movement, and manipulative skills, while participating in a non-competitive, non-threatening manner.

Come join us for a family meeting fun with opportunities for everyone to participate in non-competitive activities.

Date _____
Time _____
Place _____

Who's Invited: The whole family

We will be doing physical activities, so please dress accordingly.

Popcorn and juice will be provided after the meeting.

Please complete and detach the form below by _____ so we can reserve a space for your family.

_____ Yes, we will be off and running to attend "Get Ready, Get Set, Move!"
_____ Sorry, we will be unable to attend the meeting.

Child's name _____
Number of adults attending _____ Number of children attending _____
If you have any questions or need transportation, please call _____.

Name _____ Phone _____
Email address _____

Get Ready, Get Set, Move!

Don't forget!

We want you to "Get Ready, Get Set, Move!"
for a family meeting of movement and fun!

Date _____

Time _____

Place _____

Who's Invited: The whole family

We will be doing physical activities, so please dress
accordingly.

Popcorn and juice will be provided
after the meeting.

There's still time to RSVP. Simply send a note or call _____ as
soon as possible to reserve your spot.

Content Areas
Motor Skills
Problem Solving
Social Development

Purpose
To develop physical skills, including competency in body management and spatial movement, and manipulative skills, while participating in a non-competitive, non-threatening manner.

Note: Because this family meeting requires more space than most meetings, a large area such as a gymnasium or multi-purpose room would provide an ideal setup.

Related Books
From Head to Toe by Eric Carle
Good Thing You're Not an Octopus by Julie Markes
Here Are My Hands by Bill Martin, Jr. and John Archambault

Nametags

Materials
Red, yellow, green, blue, and orange construction paper
Scissors
Nametag patterns (see next page)
Markers

- Use the patterns (see next page) to make nametags in five colors. Make each shape a different color, such as a red beanbag, a yellow scarf, a green hoop, a blue ball, and an orange obstacle course nametag.
- Assign one color per family.
- The different colored nametags will be used to assign families to one of four activity stations.
- Make an extra set of nametags in each of the five colors to post at the activity stations.

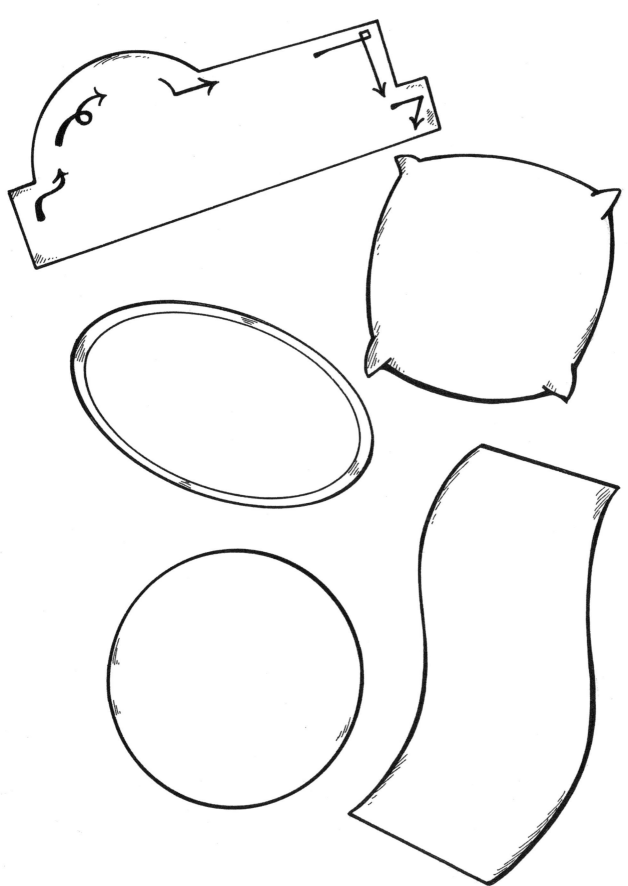

GET READY, GET SET, MOVE!

Mixer

- As families arrive, distribute the nametags.
- Ask each family member to write his or her name on the nametag and use masking tape to attach it to his or her clothing. Be sure that all members of each family have the same color nametag so they will work together at each activity station.
- Divide the families into two groups by having the people with the hoop and obstacle course nametags form a circle. Next, have the people with the ball, beanbag, and scarf nametags form a circle around the first circle so you now have two circles, one inside the other.
- Have the inside circle face the middle of the circle. Instruct the outer circle to face the other direction so the two groups are standing back to back.
- Play a CD or tape of music with a sports theme such as "Put Me in Coach" by John Fogarty. As the music plays, the inner circle should move clockwise. The outer circle should move counter-clockwise.
- Stop the music after 10 to 15 seconds. Everyone should stop moving. The two circles turn to face each other and introduce themselves.
- Repeat this process, stopping the music frequently so the families have an opportunity to introduce themselves to everyone.

Introduction

The activities in this family meeting will develop children's ability to move their bodies from one place to another (walking, running, and jumping) and to move in place (bending, twisting, pushing, and pulling). They will also increase their manipulative skills. The activities provide an opportunity to participate in physical activities in a safe, non-competitive environment.

Tell the families that their nametags will designate their activity station. If they have a beanbag nametag, they will begin at the Beanbag Station. Families are to listen for the music used in the mixer (or any other appropriate music) two minutes prior to rotation. Families are to move clockwise to the next activity station when they hear the signal. The five activity stations are:

1. Beanbags (red beanbag)
2. Scarves (yellow scarf)
3. Hoops (green hoop)
4. Balls (blue ball)
5. Create an Obstacle Course (orange obstacle course)

Family Meeting Activities

Station #1: Beanbags

(red nametag)

Using beanbags is an excellent way to develop body awareness and directional awareness.

Materials

Beanbags (1 per person)
Yarn hoops (made by tying the two ends of a long piece of yarn together so it can be made into the shape of a circle)—1 per family
6 empty, clean potato chip cans (to be used to make an obstacle course)
Note: Beanbags can be made at a minimal cost by using scrap material and rice.

What to Do

1. Try one or more of the following with your beanbag:

- Balance the beanbag on your head.
- Balance the beanbag on your foot.
- Can you balance the beanbag on other parts of your body? (knee, elbow, and other parts)
- Try walking while balancing the beanbag on the palm of your hand. Try walking while balancing the beanbag on other parts of your body.
- Can you jump while balancing the beanbag on your hand?

2. As a group, arrange the potato chip cans to make a short obstacle course. Try walking the course while balancing the beanbag on different body parts.

3. Take a yarn hoop, lay it out in the form of a circle, and complete the following tasks:

- Put your beanbags in the circle.
- Set your beanbags outside of the circle.
- Toss your beanbags in the circle.
- How close can you get your beanbags to the edge of the circle without touching the yarn?
- Walk around the outside of the yarn hoop while pushing the beanbag with your foot. Now walk around the inside of the yarn hoop while pushing the beanbag with your foot.

4. Try this beanbag challenge: How many ways can you walk around the yarn hoop while balancing your beanbag?

5. Return your beanbags and yarn hoops to their original location. Thank you!

Station #2: Scarves

(yellow nametag)

Explore the concepts of *over, under, around, in front of*, and *behind* by manipulating lightweight scarves. Introduce basic shapes and letters by making movements with the scarves. (Purchase the lightweight scarves from a department store or ask parents to donate them. Eight- to sixteen-inch square scarves are the preferred size for small hands.)

Materials
Scarves, 2 per person (or squares of lightweight material such as netting)
Box

What to Do
Prior to the meeting place all the scarves in the box.

1. Each person takes two scarves. Hold a scarf in one hand. Move your arm in a large, forward circular motion.

2. Stop and change directions so you move your arm in a backward circular motion.

3. Hold the scarf in your other hand. Move this arm in a large, forward circular motion, then change directions and move it backward.

4. Hold a scarf in each hand. Make large, forward circular motions with both hands.

5. Now make small circular motions. Reverse directions and go backward. Make fast circles, and then make slow circles.

6. Move the scarf behind your body. Can you find another way to move it behind your body?

7. Move the scarf over your body. Move the scarf under your body. Can you use your feet to move the scarf under your body?

8. Make a cape out of your scarf. Pretend you are a super hero. How does your cape move?

9. What happens if you place the scarf over your head? Can you see?

10. Play catch with your child. Carefully wad the scarf up to form a ball. Gently toss it to your child. Ask your child what happens when the scarf is tossed. Let your child try tossing the scarf to you! Repeat this activity several times.

11. Imagine there is a large piece of paper in front of you. Holding a scarf in your hand, pretend to draw different shapes (i.e., square, circle, triangle).
12. Now try "writing" different letters of the alphabet. Can you write your name?
13. Return scarves to the scarf box. Thank you!

Station #3: Hoops
(green nametag)

Develop large motor skills and balance with this activity.

Materials
6 24" hoops (If possible, have 1 hoop per family)
Beanbags

What to Do
1. Place hoops in a straight line so they are touching each other.
2. Try one or more of the following:

● Walk, placing one foot in each hoop.
● Walk, placing both feet in each hoop.
● Jump once in the first hoop, twice in the second hoop, jump once in the third hoop, jump twice in the fourth hoop, jump once in the fifth hoop, and jump twice in the sixth hoop.
● How many ways can you move in and out of the hoops? Can you be inside and outside of the hoop at the same time?

3. Roll the hoop to your child. Have your child try to roll it back to you.
4. Try spinning the hoop around your waist. Can you spin it around your arm?
5. Hold the hoop in an upright position (adult), and let the rest of your family members toss the beanbag through the hoop. Continue until each person in your family has had a turn.
6. Take the hoop challenge: How many body parts can you spin the hoop around?

Station #4: Balls

(blue nametag)

Increase ball-handling skills (manipulative skills) by using both small and large balls to provide developmentally appropriate tasks for small hands.

Materials
Yarn balls (1 for every two people)
6 12" rubber balls
6 clean, empty potato chip cans (12 if the group is large)

What to Do
1. Take turns rolling the yarn balls against the wall or large piece of cardboard.

Note: If possible, have this station situated so the children can roll and toss their balls against a wall. If a wall is not available, use a large piece of cardboard.

2. Try the above several times, and then sit in a circle with your family and take turns rolling the ball to each other.

3. After a few minutes, ask your child to toss the yarn ball to you. (A yarn ball is small, so it is easier for the children to throw, but it will be harder for them to catch. Therefore, you may wish to roll the ball back to your child rather than tossing it.)

4. Now take a 12" rubber ball. Begin by rolling the ball against the wall or cardboard. Try kicking the ball softly against the wall.

5. Once again, sit with your family in a circle. Roll the ball back and forth to each other.

6. Form a single-file line with everyone in the group. Pass the 12" rubber ball over your head from the front of the line to the end. Once the ball reaches the last person in line, that person carries the ball to the front of the line. Continue until everyone has had a chance to start the ball pass.

7. If time permits, arrange the potato chip cans so they represent bowling pins. Roll the rubber ball at the cans as if bowling. Repeat until everyone has a turn.

Note: If there are many people, use two sets of potato chip cans to cut down on waiting time.

Station #5: Create an Obstacle Course

(orange nametag)

Use creativity to work cooperatively to design an obstacle course. After the design is complete take the challenge of completing the course!

Materials

Smooth board to use as balance beam
24" hoops, two or three
Beanbag chairs or large pillows
Large boxes to make tunnels
Pieces of construction paper to use as stepping stones
Tape
Paper and pencils

What to Do

1. As a group, discuss the options for making an obstacle course using the materials provided. Sketch out the course if desired.
2. Once a course has been decided upon, work cooperatively to construct your obstacle course.
3. After constructing your design, try the challenge of completing the course!

Invite the families for an after-meeting snack of popcorn and juice after completing an evaluation form.

EVALUATION

Get Ready, Get Set, Move!

Family Meeting Evaluation

We hope you have had an evening of fun with your family and friends. Please let us know what you thought of tonight's activities. Your thoughts and comments about the meeting are valuable to us. Circle one of the following.

Off and running with a great meeting!

Slow down and take a minute to rethink the game plan.

Definite scratch— try again.

Comments and Suggestions

_____
_____
_____
_____
_____

Thank you for coming!

The Great Graphing Safari

Come with us and explore the world of graphing!

Join the fun as we collect information and graph it in a variety of ways. We will make all types of graphs, including pictographs and living graphs!

So come along on our safari and discover the exciting world of graphing!

Date _____
Time _____
Place _____

Who's Invited: The whole family

Dress comfortably for a night of fun!

Refreshments will be served.

Please complete and detach the form below by _____ so we can reserve a space for your family.

_____ Yes, we will attend "The Great Graphing Safari."
_____ Sorry, we will be unable to attend the meeting.

Child's name _____
Number of adults attending _____ Number of children attending _____

If you have any questions or need transportation, please call _____.

Name _____ Phone _____

Email address _____

The Great Graphing Safari

Just a reminder!

The Great Graphing Safari is approaching quickly!

Date _____

Time _____

Place _____

Who's Invited: The whole family

Please dress comfortably (Yes, we will be painting!) and bring the whole family for a night of fun.

Refreshments will be served.

Please call _____ to RSVP as soon as possible if you haven't sent in your reservation form.

We still have room for more!

© Gryphon House, Inc. 800.638.0928 www.gryphonhouse.com
Publisher permits photocopying of this page for distribution

Content Areas

Literacy
Math
Problem Solving
Social Development

Purpose

To present a range of activities that offer opportunities to collect, share, and compare information using graphs, and to reinforce counting, letter recognition, and fine motor skills.

Related Books

Castles, Caves, and Honeycombs by Linda Ashman (home preference)
Chicka Chicka Boom Boom by Bill Martin, Jr. and John Archambault
   (naming)
The Colors of Us by Karen Katz (personal physical qualities)
Houses and Homes by Ann Morris (home and food preferences)
I Love My Hair by Natasha Anastasia Tarpley (personal physical qualities)
We All Sing with the Same Voice by J. Philip Miller and Sheppard M. Greene
   (personal physical abilities)

Nametags

Materials
Construction paper
Scissors
Safari hat pattern (see next page)
Small animal stickers (five different types—lions, elephants, giraffes, zebras,
   and rhinoceros are possible choices)
Markers

- Use the safari hat pattern (see next page) to make nametags.
- Put one animal sticker on each nametag. The animals will let the
   participants know at which station they will begin.
- Assign one animal per family.
- Make an extra set of nametags using the five animal stickers to post at
   the activity stations.

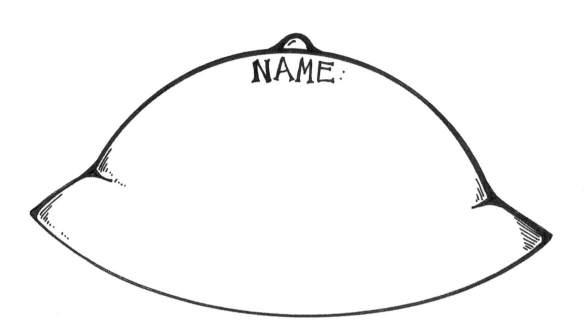

NAME:

Mixer

- As families arrive, distribute the nametags.
- Ask each family member to write his or her name on the nametag and use masking tape to attach it to his or her clothing.
- Be sure that all members of each family have the same animal sticker nametag so they will work together at each activity station.
- Ask the families to go to the station designated by the animal on their nametag. Once they are at their station, families should be encouraged to visit as they wait for everyone to register. While they are getting to know other members in their group, they will be asked to decide what their favorite animal is.
- Ask if any group selected a dog as its favorite animal. Those who did will form a line in a designated area. Then ask who selected the horse as their favorite animal. These people will form another line next to the previously formed line.
- Continue until four lines are formed. Possible animal choices for the two remaining lines may include a cat, monkey, or bear. If all participants are not in a line after four choices are offered, ask the remaining participants to please form a line.
- Explain that they have just formed a living graph. Based on this graph, decide which animal was selected the most and which was selected the least number of times.

Introduction

During this family meeting the participants collect data regarding personal qualities, food and home preferences, clothing, and names at the five activity stations. After collecting and recording the information, they will graph the results in a variety of ways and compare the findings. The graphs will include bar graphs, pictographs, and living graphs.

Tell the families that they are to begin at the activity station that matches the animal on their nametag. For example, if there is a lion on their nametag, they begin at the Lion Station. If they have an elephant on their nametag, they begin at the Elephant Station, and so on. When the lights flicker the first time, there will be two to three minutes to straighten up the station. When the lights flicker the second time, move clockwise to the next activity station. The five activity stations are:

1. I Am Special (lion sticker)
2. There's No Place Like Home (elephant sticker)
3. And the Winner Is… (giraffe sticker)
4. The Name Game (zebra sticker)
5. The Great Graphing Literacy Center (rhinoceros sticker)

Family Meeting Activities

Station #1: I Am Special

(lion sticker nametag)

This station provides an opportunity to share and compare physical qualities.

Materials
3" x 5" index cards
Birthday cake patterns (one for each person)
Pencils
Markers
Glue
Graphs (see sample on pages 156-157)

What to Do
(At this activity station there will be two graphing activities—one by hair type [straight, wavy, or curly] and one by birthday month.)

1. Write your name on a 3 x 5 index card.
2. Use a colored marker to write your hair type (straight, wavy, or curly) on the card.
3. Tape or glue the index card in the column representing their hair type.
4. Write the month of your birthday on a birthday cake pattern. Glue or tape the patterns in the column of the month you were born.
5. Discuss results of the graphs. How many qualities do you share with another person? Do you have the same hair type and color? How many people have a birthday in the same month as you? Which month contains the most birthdays?

Station #2: There's No Place Like Home

(elephant sticker nametag)

Discover different kinds of homes people might live in and construct an ideal home.

Materials

Large graph for recording the group's data
Chart paper
Markers
Building materials (possible suggestions include building blocks, paper towel tubes, small boxes, and Legos)
Graph (see sample on page 158)

What to Do

1. As a group, brainstorm and list various types of homes people might live in. Possible types of homes might include castles, tents, treehouses, and caves.
2. Select five to place on the graph and put the names of these homes on the graph.
3. As a family, decide which one of the five types of homes you would like to live in.
4. As a family, construct the home you selected with blocks, Legos, and other building materials.
5. Share your home building ideas with the group at your station.

Station #3: And the Winner Is…

(giraffe sticker nametag)

Determine which color of M&Ms appears most frequently and graph the results.

Materials

Plain M&Ms
Baggies
Napkins or paper towels
Copies of the graph (see page 159)
$1/3$ measuring cup
Graph (see sample on page 159)

What to Do

1. Each person measures ⅓ cup of M&Ms and places them on a napkin.
2. Count the M&Ms. Sort them by color.
3. Each person places his or her M&Ms in the appropriate color row on a copy of the graph.
4. Compare the number of each color of M&Ms with other family members.
5. Put your M&Ms in a baggie so you can eat them as part of the snack after the workshop.

Station #4: The Name Game

(zebra sticker nametag)

Form several living graphs using information from the names of the family members.

Materials

Alphabet letters taped along the wall

What to Do

1. Each participant introduces him- or herself to the group, stating his or her first, middle, and last name.
2. Stand under the alphabet letter that is the first letter in your first name. Help children find the right spot, if necessary.
3. After all the children are standing under the correct letter, all the adults find the letter of the alphabet that their first name begins with and add themselves to this "people" graph.
4. Count the number of people in each line (for each letter).
5. Discuss which letter occurs at the beginning of names most frequently and least frequently within their group. Does anyone have the same name? How many more names begin with one letter compared to another?
6. Complete steps 2 through 6 using the first initial of everyone's middle name.
7. Repeat the same process using the first initial of everyone's last name.

Station #5: The Great Graphing Literacy Center

(rhinoceros sticker nametag)

Make a pictograph representing colors of clothing.

Materials
Mary Wore Her Red Dress by Merle Peek
Copies of the patterns of various pieces of clothing (see page 154)
Large graph made from chart paper
Crayons
Scissors
Graph (see sample on page 160)

What to Do
(Prior to the family meeting, post a large piece of chart paper on the wall.
Draw columns for each of the clothing items in the illustration on the next
page.)

1. One person from the group reads *Mary Wore Her Red Dress* written by
   Merle Peek.
2. Select patterns of clothing representing what you are wearing. For
   example, if you are wearing jeans and a shirt, take a pattern of pants
   and a shirt. If you are wearing a dress, take a pattern of a dress.
3. Color the pattern to match the outfit you are wearing. If you are
   wearing a blue dress, you will color the pattern of the dress blue.
4. Cut out the patterns you colored.
5. As a family, go up to the graph together and place your clothing
   patterns in the appropriate color column.

Thank everyone for coming and invite them to enjoy a snack of pretzels
and juice, along with their M&Ms, after completing the evaluation.

THE GREAT GRAPHING SAFARI

EVALUATION

The Great Graphing Safari

Family Meeting Evaluation

We would like to know what you thought of tonight's meeting. Your comments are important to us and help us as we plan future meetings. Thank you for your time.

Please color the bar that indicates how you liked our meeting!

Comments and Suggestions

_____

_____

_____

_____

_____

_____

_____

Thank you for coming!

Hair Type

Straight	Wavy	Curly

Birthday Month

J	F	M	A	M	J	J	A	S	O	N	D

THE GREAT GRAPHING SAFARI

Type of Home

M&M Preference

Clothing

THE GREAT GRAPHING SAFARI

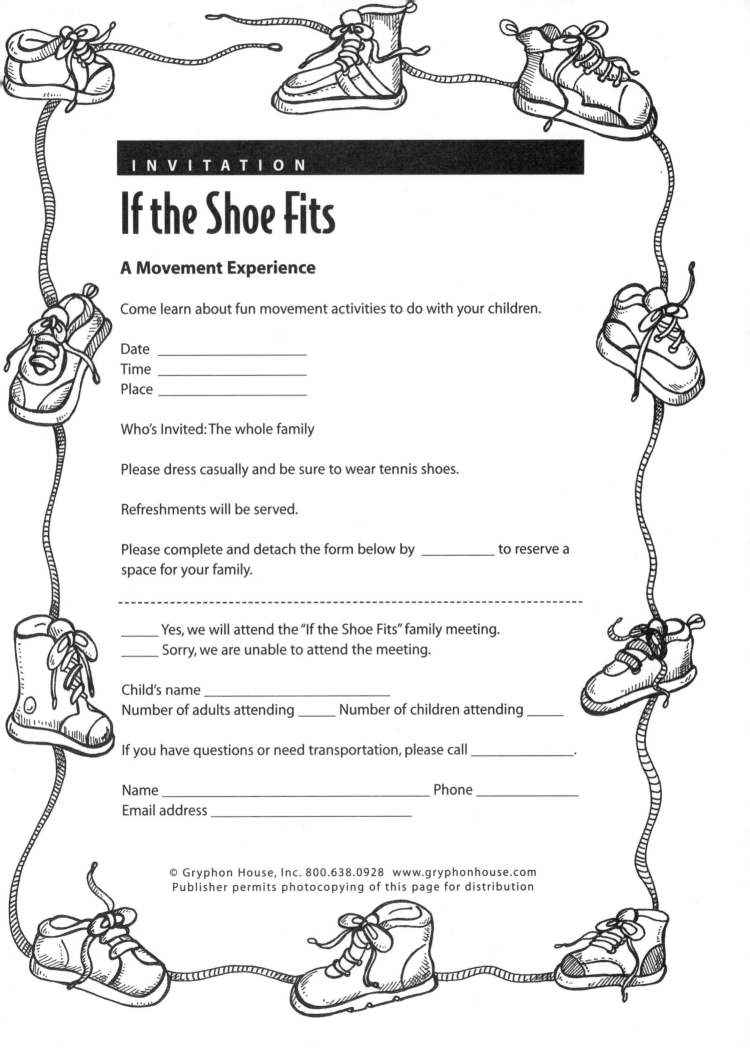

If the Shoe Fits

A Movement Experience

Come learn about fun movement activities to do with your children.

Date _____

Time _____

Place _____

Who's Invited: The whole family

Please dress casually and be sure to wear tennis shoes.

Refreshments will be served.

Please complete and detach the form below by _____ to reserve a space for your family.

- -

_____ Yes, we will attend the "If the Shoe Fits" family meeting.
_____ Sorry, we are unable to attend the meeting.

Child's name _____

Number of adults attending _____ Number of children attending _____

If you have questions or need transportation, please call _____.

Name _____ Phone _____
Email address _____

If the Shoe Fits

Just a reminder!

Don't miss our "If the Shoe Fits" family meeting.

Date _____

Time _____

Place _____

Who's Invited: The whole family

Please dress casually and be sure to wear tennis shoes.

Refreshments will be served.

There is still time to reserve a spot for you and your family.

Just call _____ and let us know who is coming.

Content Areas

Motor Skills
Music and Movement
Problem Solving
Social Development

Purpose

To develop an awareness of fundamental movement skills through
activities that families can do together.

Nametags

Materials

Tennis shoe pattern (see next page)
Paper
Marker
Scissors
Construction paper
Glue or tape
Hole punch
Yarn—red, green, yellow and blue

- Outline tennis shoe features with a black marker. Cut out the shoe.
- Glue or paste the tennis shoe to a piece of construction paper and cut
  out. This will make a sturdy nametag.
- Punch holes for the shoelaces.
- Use four different colors of yarn (red, green, yellow, and blue). These
  colors will correspond to those at each of the four activity stations.
- Lace the tennis shoes with the yarn.
- Make an extra set of nametags in each of the four colors to post at the
  activity stations.

Mixer

- Greet families as they arrive and distribute the nametags.
- Ask each family member to write his or her name on a nametag and use masking tape to attach it to his or her clothing.
- Be sure all members of each family have nametags with the same color shoelaces so they can work together at each activity station.
- Tell them that you are going to trade them a nametag for one of the tennis shoes each is wearing.
- Put all the collected shoes in a large box.
- After families have arrived, ask them to form a large circle.
- Dump the box of collected tennis shoes into a pile in the center of the circle.
- Explain that each person is to go to the pile and select one shoe, except that it cannot be his or her own shoe or belong to a member of their family.

- After everyone has selected a shoe, participants try to find the individual who owns that shoe.
- Once they find that person, they ask each other a question, such as:

  - If you could be any piece of sports equipment, what would you be?
  - What is your favorite sport to watch?
  - What is your favorite sport to play?
  - Who is your favorite player?
  - What was your favorite sport when you were a child?

Introduction

During the early childhood years, children learn to move and move to learn. Movement and learning go hand in hand. Learning to move is part of the continuous development of children's basic movement abilities, which establish the foundation for more complex movement skills as the children move on to the elementary school years. Three-, four-, and five-year-olds are at the initial stages of motor development. Between the ages of 6 and 10, children will apply these movement skills to sports, games, and dancing. The fundamental movement skills are walking, running, jumping, skipping, rolling, throwing, catching, kicking, stretching, bending, twisting, and shaking. Balance, rhythm, and coordination are essential components.

Warming up before you do any exercise or physical activity reduces the risk of injury by stretching your muscles and getting the blood flowing through the body. Swinging arms, jogging in place slowly, and doing easy stretching movements are fun ways to get the heart pumping.

Prepare for the next activities by warming up together. Form a large circle. Take two giant steps apart to give everyone enough room to move without bumping into someone else. Do the following movements together:

1. Shrug your shoulders up and down four times.
2. Roll your shoulders forward four times.
3. Roll your shoulders back four times.
4. Raise both arms out from your side. Circle arms forward four times.
5. Raise both arms out from your side and circle backward four times.
6. Slowly jog in place and count to 20.
7. Raise both arms up over your head and reach for the ceiling. Hold for a count of four.

8. Stand tall and slowly bend over as far as possible without bending your knees. Raise up slowly.

9. Put your right hand on your left shoulder and twist your neck to the right, looking back as far as possible.

10. Place your left hand on your right shoulder and twist your neck to the left looking back as far as possible.

11. Take a slow deep breath in through your nose (inhale). Now slowly breathe out through your mouth (exhale). Repeat two times.

12. Now wrap your arms around yourself and give yourself a big hug!

Everyone should be warmed up and feeling loose. Tell families to look at their nametags. Those with red shoelaces should walk to the red station, green shoelaces to the green station, and so on.

1. Body Balance (red shoelaces)
2. Let's Go to the Beach (green shoelaces)
3. Walk to the Beat (yellow shoelaces)
4. Ball Toss (blue shoelaces)

Families will move clockwise from the first activity station to the next when room lights are turned off and on.

Family Meeting Activities

Station #1: Body Balance

(red shoelaces nametag)

Coordination and balance are important components of the 12 basic movement skills. This activity contributes to movement skill development, while allowing for different ability levels as well as creativity and problem solving.

Materials

None

What to Do

1. Do as many of the following as time permits:

- Make a bridge using four parts of your body.
- Make your bridge as high as possible.
- Make your bridge as low as possible.
- Make your bridge as wide as possible.
- Make your bridge as narrow as possible.
- Make a bridge using only three parts of the body.
- Make a bridge using two parts of your body.
- Hop two times on one foot.
- Hop two times on the other foot.
- Put your feet together and take two big jumps forward.
- Put your feet together and take two big jumps backward.
- Take two little jumps forward and two backward.
- Take three jumps forward in a zigzag pattern.
- Stand on one foot and make your body as tall as possible.
- Stand on one foot and make your body as small as possible.
- With your feet wide apart, take two jumps forward, then two jumps back.
- Standing in one place, jump as high as you can three times.
- Now jump in one place three times as you clap your hands.
- Stand in one place and get as low as you can with your entire body.

2. Collaborate with members of your family or with other members of the group as you create solutions to the instructions.

Station #2: Let's Go to the Beach

(green shoelaces nametag)

Children become more adept at these skills as they use them repeatedly during play. This type of activity is called creative movement because it allows us to express ourselves creatively as we move.

Materials

Large, open space

What to Do

1. One person (a facilitator or one of the parents) tells the following story and everyone else acts out the movements described in the story.

We're going to take a trip to the beach. Let's start walking. Ah! I can see the sand and the water. Let's take off our shoes and run to the water. Jump into the water with both feet. The water is getting deeper. What kind of steps do we need to take? Yes! Big high steps. Step as high as you can. Look at the sailboat! The people on the boat are waving. Wave back! Let's swim back to the beach. Oh, that sand feels so wet and cool. Let's lie down and rest for a second. Why don't we roll in it a few times? Let's stand up now. Shake your whole body to get the sand off. Now, curl your toes in the sand. See your footprints? Let's make some more footprints. What other kinds of footprints can you make? Step heavy and make some deep footprints. Now, let's step softly and try to not make any footprints at all. Let's see how far apart we can make our footprints. Walk like a giant in the sand. What kind of foot prints do you think ants would leave in the sand? Little ones. Let's take little steps like ants. It's time to go home. Let's skip or gallop (three's and four's may be to young to skip) back to the bus. We're back! Wasn't that fun?

Station #3: Walk to the Beat

(yellow shoelaces nametag)

Develops the fundamental skills of walking, rhythm, and coordination.

Materials

Variety of music selections with a moderate beat, such as "When the Saints Go Marching In," "Yellow Submarine," or "So Long, It's Been Good to Know You"

What to Do

1. As a group, form a large circle, turn to the right, listen, and respond to the following walking patterns called out by a facilitator or parent.

- Walk forward. Stop!
- Walk backward. Stop!
- Walk with teeny, tiny steps. Stop!
- Walk with giant steps. Stop!
- Walk forward with your hands behind your back. Stop!
- Walk slowly. Stop!
- Walk on your tiptoes. Stop!
- Walk on your heels. Stop!
- Walk with stiff knees and arms. Stop!
- Walk as low as you can. Stop!
- Walk as tall as you can. Stop!
- Turn around and walk while clapping your hands. Stop!
- Walk like you're in water that's reaching your knees. Stop!
- Walk like you're angry. Stop!
- Walk like you're tired. Stop!
- Walk like you're happy. Stop!
- Walk to the beat of the caller as he or she claps his or her hands.

2. Take turns being the caller.

Station #4: Ball Toss
(blue shoelaces nametag)

Throwing and catching are difficult skills for young children. Catching yarn or foam balls is much easier and safer than catching hard balls. Throwing and catching require coordination between hands and eyes as well as between feet and eyes.

Materials
Assortment of colored yarn or soft foam balls
Large sturdy cardboard box with target cut in the side (could be a clown face with cutouts of eyes, nose, and mouth large enough for the soft balls to enter when thrown)

What to Do
Before the family meeting, prepare the box by drawing a target and cutting out a variety of holes in the target.
1. Each family will need a ball.
2. Try the following throw-and-catch variations:

- Take turns throwing the ball up in the air and catching it with two hands.
- Throw the ball up and catch it with one hand.
- Throw the ball in the air and clap one time before it comes down to the floor.
- Stand about four feet from each other and throw the ball underhand to a family member. Move closer or farther away to practice changing the force of the throw.
- Throw the ball up and turn around before it comes down. Can you catch it?

3. Stand at an appropriate distance from the target and throw the balls at it.

Cool Down—Whole Group Activity

1. Sit or lie down on the floor.
2. Take a deep breath and hold it for a count of five. Let it out slowly.
3. Take another deep breath and hold it for a count of five. Let it out slowly.
4. Stand up. Swing your arms in a large circle for a count of five. Now, let your arms hang limp and relaxed.
5. Roll your shoulder back five times. Roll your shoulders forward five times.
7. Take a deep breath. Hold it for a count of five and let your breath out with a whoosh!
8. Take another deep breath. Hold it for a count of five and let it out with a whoosh!
9. Remain quiet and relaxed for 30 seconds.

Thank everyone for coming and invite them to share a snack of seasonal fruit and crackers after completing the evaluation forms.

EVALUATION

If the Shoe Fits

Family Meeting Evaluation

There are three tennis shoes on this evaluation form. One shoe is laced, another is half-laced, and another is untied. Please circle the shoe that you feel best fits our meeting. Also, please add any comments you wish to share with us in the space provided.

How did we do?

Comments and Suggestions

_____

_____

_____

_____

_____

_____

_____

Thank you for coming!

INVITATION

Let's Monkey Around!

Please join us for an evening of fun as we "go bananas" sharing monkey stories, creating masks, singing songs, and doing fingerplays.

Come along for an evening of family fun!

Date _____

Time _____

Place _____

Who's Invited: The whole family

Snacks will be served!

Please dress comfortably!

Please complete and detach the form below by _____ to reserve a space for your family.

- -

_____ Yes, we will attend the "Let's Monkey Around" family meeting.

_____ Sorry, we are unable to attend the meeting.

Child's name _____

Number of adults attending _____ Number of children attending _____

If you have questions or need transportation, please call _____.

Name _____ Phone _____

Email address _____

Special thanks to the students in CI 421, Child, Family, and Community Relationships, at Southern Illinois University—Edwardsville, Spring 2002.

Let's Monkey Around!

Just in case it slipped your mind…

Our next family meeting, "Let's Monkey Around," is approaching quickly.

Date _____

Time _____

Place _____

Who's Invited : The whole family

Snacks will be served!

Please dress comfortably!

There is still time to reserve a spot for you and your family.

Just call _____ and let us know how many people will be coming.

Content Areas
Art
Literacy
Music

Purpose
To promote family involvement while encouraging creativity through children's literature.

Nametags

Materials
Red, blue, orange, and green
  construction paper
Scissors
Monkey pattern (at right)
Markers

- Use the monkey pattern (at right) to make nametags in four colors.
- Assign one color per family.
- Different colored nametags will be used to assign families to one of four activity stations.
- Make an extra set of nametags in each of the four colors to post at the activity stations.

Mixer
- As families arrive, distribute the monkey nametags.
- Ask each family member to write his or her name on the nametag and use masking tape to attach it to his or her clothing.
- Be sure all members of each family have the same color nametag so they will work together at each activity station.
- Give each person a copy of the "Curious George" game board (page 183) and a pencil or pen.

174

- Explain that the evening will begin with a short activity to help everyone get acquainted.
- Instruct participants to walk around the room to find people with the characteristics listed on the spaces of the game board.
- When they find someone with one of the characteristics, that person needs to sign or initial that particular block. A person can only sign one space per sheet.
- Play music or flick the lights to signal the beginning and end of the activity.

Introduction

Ask everyone who was able to fill in all of the spaces on their game card to stand up and receive a round of applause. The activities in this family meeting use some of the children's favorite monkey stories. Encourage everyone to "monkey" around!

Tell the families to go to the activity station that matches the color of their nametags. (Point out the location of each activity station.) When they see the lights flickering, it is time to start cleaning up the activity station. When the lights flicker again, it is time to move clockwise to the next activity station. At the end of the evening, there will be a final activity for the entire group. The four activity stations are:

1. Silly Monkey Mask (red monkey)
2. Five Little Monkeys Jumping on the Bed (blue monkey)
3. Monkey Finger Puppets (orange monkey)
4. Fingerplay of "Five Little Monkeys Jumping on the Bed" (green monkey)

Family Meeting Activities

Station #1—Silly Monkey Mask

(red monkey nametag)

Materials

Pre-cut monkey masks made of brown construction paper with eyes cut out, one for each participant

Hole punchers

Yarn

Crayons

What to Do

1. Help your child punch a hole in each side of the mask and tie a piece of yarn in each hole.
2. Encourage your child to decorate his or her mask with crayons.
3. When the masks are finished, the children wear their masks and pretend to be monkeys.

Station #2: Five Little Monkeys Jumping on the Bed (blue monkey nametag)

Materials
Five Little Monkeys Jumping on the Bed by Eileen Christelow (use the
 Big Book if possible)
Flannel board and flannel characters

What to Do
Before the meeting, make flannel board pieces for this story using the
illustrations on this page and next.

1. Select an adult to read the book to the families at this activity station.
   The reader should be encouraged to use different voices for the characters, follow the singsong rhythm of the story, and show the pictures in
   the book to the participants while reading.
2. Read the story again, using the flannel board. Ask the children to help
   with the characters on the flannel board.

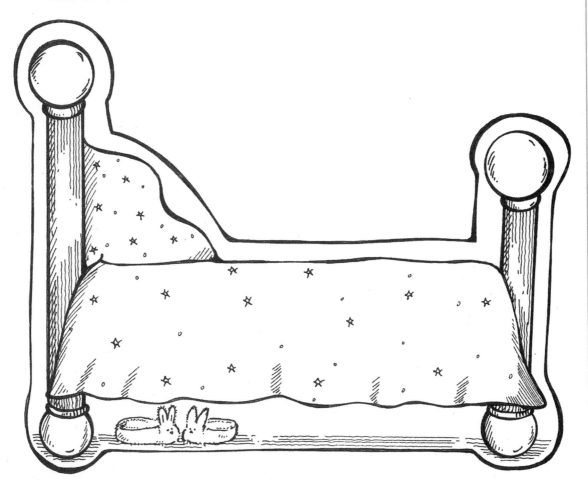

LET'S MONKEY AROUND!

177

LET'S MONKEY AROUND!

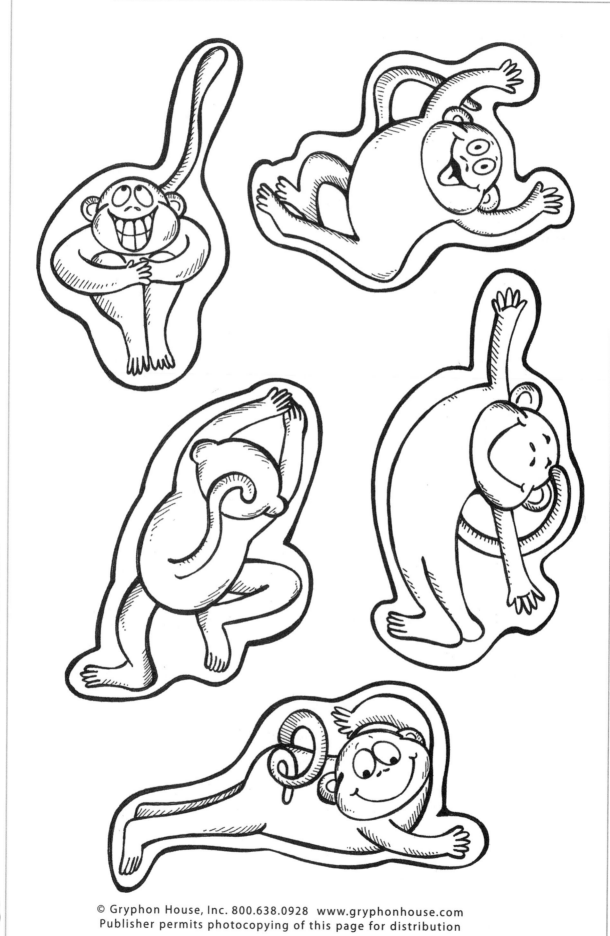

Station #3: Monkey Finger Puppets

(orange nametag)

Note: The activity at this station requires cutting five puppets per person. It would be helpful if volunteers could help cut the puppets before the meeting.

Materials
Pre-cut monkey puppets—(5 for each participant)
Washable markers
Tape

What to Do
1. Color each monkey with markers.
2. Wrap and tape each monkey around each of your fingers.
3. Use the puppets at station #4 or during the closing activity.

Station #4: Fingerplay of "Five Little Monkeys Jumping on the Bed"

(green nametag)

Materials
CD* with "Five Little Monkeys" fingerplay

What to Do
1. Play the first verse of the fingerplay. (If necessary, ask the teacher or facilitator to demonstrate the actions.)
2. Join in the actions for the remaining verses.
3. If time permits, repeat the fingerplay.

Group Activity—"Monkey See, Monkey Do"

Ask the families to return to the center of the room. Play the song "Monkey See, Monkey Do" (by Renah Wolzinger on Tumble-n-Tunes CD) and have the families sing along while wearing their monkey masks or using their monkey finger puppets.

Thank the families for coming. Ask the families to fill out an evaluation sheet and invite them to share refreshments. A "monkey" snack idea: dried bananas and juice.

*Five Little Monkeys: Songs for Singing and Playing, Available from Kimbo Educational, www.kimboed.com, 800-632-2187.

EVALUATION

Let's Monkey Around!

Family Meeting Evaluation

We are interested in knowing what you thought of tonight's meeting. Please circle one of the following sets of bananas that best describes your thoughts. Feel free to add additional comments at the bottom of the page. Thank you.

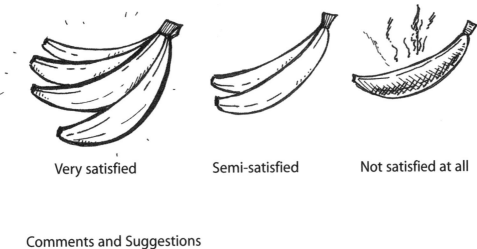

Very satisfied   Semi-satisfied   Not satisfied at all

Comments and Suggestions

_____

_____

_____

_____

_____

_____

_____

_____

_____

Thank you for coming!

MORE MONKEY BOOKS

Books About the *Five Little Monkeys* by Eileen Christelow

Five Little Monkeys Jumping on the Bed
Five Little Monkeys Sitting in a Tree
Five Little Monkeys Wash the Car
Five Little Monkeys With Nothing to Do

Books About *Curious George* by H.A. Rey and Margret Rey

Complete Adventures of Curious George
Curious George Goes Camping

New Adventures of *Curious George*

Curious George ABCs
Curious George and the Dinosaur
Curious George and the Dump Truck
Curious George and the Puppies
Curious George at the Parade
Curious George Gets a Medal
Curious George Goes to School
Curious George Goes to the Beach
Curious George Goes to the Movie
Curious George in the Hot Air Balloon
Curious George in the Snow
Curious George Learns the Alphabet
Curious George Makes Pancakes
Curious George Opposites
Curious George Plays Baseball
Curious George Visits the Zoo
Curious George's Dream

Additional Monkey Books

Caps for Sale by Esphyr Slobodkina
Chimp and Zee by Catherine Anholt
Do Monkeys Tweet? by Melanie Walsh
Hug by Jez Alborough
I Am a Little Monkey by Francois Crozat
Little Red Monkey by Jonathan London
The Missing Bananas by Richard Scarry
Ten Little Monkeys by Keith Faulkner

Are You as Curious as George?

Instructions
Walk around the room to find people with these characteristics. When you find someone with a particular characteristic, ask him or her to sign that block. Try to fill every space within the time allowed. Remember, a person can only sign one space per sheet.

Find someone with brown hair	Find someone with blue eyes	Find someone wearing a red shirt
Find someone wearing glasses	FREE SPACE (picture of Curious George)	Find someone wearing a hat
Find someone wearing earrings	Find someone wearing nail polish	Find someone wearing shoes with heels

Magical Art Mixtures

Come learn about magical art mixtures that you can brew at home!

Date _____
Time _____
Place _____

Who's Invited: The whole family

Dress: Casual. Bring old paint shirts and smocks if you can. (Washable paints will be used.)

Refreshments will be served.

Please complete and detach the form below by _____ to reserve a space for your family.

_____ Yes, we will attend the "Magical Art Mixtures" family meeting.
_____ Sorry, we are unable to attend the meeting.

Child's name _____
Number of adults attending _____ Number of children attending _____

If you have questions or need transportation, please call _____.

Name _____ Phone _____
Email address _____

Magical Art Mixtures

Don't forget about our Magical Art Mixtures family meeting!

Date _____
Time _____
Place _____

Who's Invited: The whole family

Dress: Casual. Bring old paint shirts and smocks if you can. (Washable paints will be used.)

Refreshments will be served.

If you haven't made reservations for your family, please call _____ as soon as possible.

Content Areas
Art
Motor Skills
Science

Purpose
To provide families with "recipes" of art activities that can be done at home using mixtures and common household ingredients.

Related Books
Cool Ali by Nancy Poydar
Mouse Painting by Ellen Stoll Walsh

Nametags

Materials
Blank recipe cards (or index cards) in green, blue, red and yellow
Masking tape
Markers or crayons

- Assign one color recipe (or index) card per family.
- Different colored nametags will be used to assign families to one of four activity stations.
- Make an extra set of nametags to post at activity stations.

Mixer—"Getting to Know You" Bingo

- As families arrive, distribute the nametags.
- Ask family members to write their names on nametags and use masking tape to attach the nametags to their clothing.
- Be sure that all members of each family have the same color nametag so they can work together at each activity station.
- Give each family a Bingo card (see page 192) and a pencil.
- Explain that they are to move about the room and interact with the other families to find someone who has done one of the activities on the Bingo card. When they find someone, they will ask that person to sign his or her name in that space on the Bingo card. They should get a different signature for each space. The center space is a "free" space that can be filled in with the family name.

Introduction

Children enjoy expressing themselves through art and are more interested in the process of art than in the finished product. Art provides experiences that allow children to explore their senses, feel a sense of accomplishment, and enjoy creative expression. The activities in this family meeting are filled with creative ways to explore with paint that can easily be done at home.

Tell the families to go to the activity station that matches the color of their nametags. Those with the yellow colored nametags will start at the yellow activity station. Those with the red will begin at the red station, and so on. When they hear a timer bell, it is time to move clockwise to the next activity station. The four activity stations are:

1. String Painting (yellow nametag)
2. Bubble Paint (red nametag)
3. Soap Finger Painting (blue nametag)
4. Wet Chalk Creations (green nametag)

Remind families that the art masterpieces created at this family meeting will be saved and sent home when they are dry. Therefore, it is essential that all the artists sign their masterpieces.

Family Meeting Activities

Station #1: String Painting

(yellow nametag)

Extend knowledge of the physical world with these three-dimensional designs.

Materials

Paper
Liquid starch
Liquid tempera paint
Variety of different length strings and yarns
Paint containers (recycled margarine tubs are great)
Newspapers or paint drop cloths to manage spills
Sponges and paper towels for cleaning up

What to Do

1. Working as a group, mix equal parts of liquid starch and liquid tempera paint in a paint container. Create three or four different colors.
2. Dip a length of string or yarn into one of the tempera and liquid starch mixtures.
3. Drag the string across the paper. Make any design you wish.
4. Hold the string vertically above the paper and let it drop.
5. The starch in the liquid tempera will cause the string to adhere to the paper as it dries.
6. Clean up the area so it is ready for the next group.

Station #2: Bubble Paint

(red nametag)

Discover a new way to create art without brushes.

Materials

Bubble mixture (see recipe on next page)
Large containers
Food coloring
Bubble blowers (commercial or homemade from pipe cleaners, fruit containers, or straws)
4 easels
Paper

What to Do

1. Working as a group, make four containers of bubble mixture. Put one container on or near each easel.
2. (One family works at each easel.) Dip bubble blowers into the mixture.
3. Stand two feet back from the easel.
4. Blow bubbles forward onto the paper.
5. Bubbles pop, leaving a colored imprint on the paper.
6. Remove and allow to dry.
7. Clean up the area so it is ready for the next group.

Recipe for Bubble Mixture

$\frac{1}{3}$ cup (75mL) liquid dishwashing soap (Dawn® is best)
1 cup (250mL) water
1 tablespoon (15mL) sugar
Food coloring

Mix together in large containers. Add a different color of food coloring to each container.

Station #3: Soap Fingerpainting
(blue nametag)

Materials

Large mixing bowl
Soap flakes
Measuring tablespoon and cups
Hand or electric mixer
Large spoons
Variety of dark colored, textured wallpaper (use old wallpaper books from paint stores)
Paper towels
Water source to wash hands

What to Do

1. Working as a group, make soap fingerpaint by pouring 1 cup (250mL) soap flakes into the large bowl. Add 4 tablespoons (60ml) of water. Double or triple recipe, if needed.
2. Use the mixer (adults only) to whip the soap flakes and water mixture to the consistency of frosting. Add food coloring if desired. (Use white paper rather than wallpaper if using food coloring.)

3. Use the large spoons to place some of the soap flake mixture onto your sheet of wallpaper.
4. Use your fingers and hands to make a fingerpaint creation.
5. Rinse hands in water and dry.
6. Clean up the area so it is ready for the next group.

Station #4: Wet Chalk Creations

(green nametag)

The tactile effect of wet chalk easily leaving marks is fascinating.

Materials
Colored chalk
Water
Sugar
Measuring spoons
Bowls
Mixing spoons
Paper towels
Newspapers to place under the paper as a pad
Water source or container of water for washing hands
Fixative (optional)

What to Do
1. Working as a group, mix a solution of 1 teaspoon (5mL) sugar and 1 tablespoon (15mL) water. Stir until it is the consistency of oil-based paint. Double or triple this recipe mixture as necessary.
2. Dip the colored chalk into the sugar and water mixture and draw with the chalk on the paper.
3. After the chalk creation dries, it can be sprayed with a fixative (adults only) to prevent smearing.
4. Clean up the area so it is ready for the next group.
Hint: When a thin coating of film appears on the chalk after repeated rubbing, rub the end with fine sandpaper or steel wool.

Thank everyone for coming and ask them to complete an evaluation form before sharing a snack of seasonal fruit and crackers.

Magical Art Mixtures

Family Meeting Evaluation

We want to know what you think about the meeting this evening. Please circle the measuring cup that best describes your feelings. Use the space at the bottom of the page if you wish to make a comment.

Lots of fun with lots of ideas!

Good time—a few ideas

O.K.—an idea or two

Comments and Suggestions

_____

_____

_____

_____

_____

_____

_____

Thank you for coming!

"Getting to Know You" Bingo

Create one Bingo card for each family. If desired, put different family activities on each card. The center space is "free." The family activities to write in the other spaces include:

- Ate breakfast together this morning
- Baked cookies recently
- Read a bedtime story last night
- Used measuring cups today
- Drank no soda today
- Ate pizza this week
- Exercised together
- Drew a picture this week
- Played a game together
- Mailed a letter at the post office
- Went to the library
- Colored together

- Played at the park
- Went for a walk
- Made and drank hot chocolate
- Made some popcorn this week
- Sang a song together
- Put a puzzle together
- Fingerpainted together
- Blew bubbles
- Ate ice cream
- Went swimming
- Made lemonade
- Listened to music

MAGICAL ART MIXTURES

Meaningful Math

All families are welcome to the "Meaningful Math" family meeting!

Your family is invited to a fun-filled family meeting that will give everyone an opportunity to learn how daily activities at home and at school can help children to develop positive attitudes about math.

Date _____

Time _____

Place _____

Who's Invited: The whole family

Dress: Casual

Refreshments will be served.

Please complete and detach the form below by _____ to reserve a space for your family.

_____ Yes, we will attend the "Meaningful Math" family meeting.
_____ Sorry, we are unable to attend the meeting.

Child's name _____

Number of adults attending _____ Number of children attending _____

If you have questions or need transportation, please call _____.

Name _____ Phone _____
Email address _____

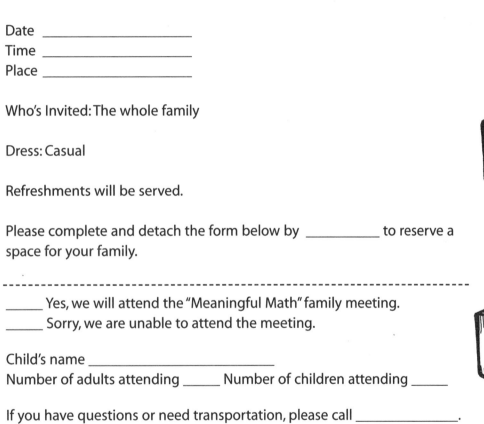

Meaningful Math

Don't Forget!

Your family is invited to join us for Meaningful Math hands-on activities.

It's sure to add a big plus to your day!

Date _____
Time _____
Place _____

Who's Invited: The whole family

Dress: Casual

Refreshments will be served.

Come for a family meeting of fun and socializing while we work together on math activities that are appropriate for both home and school.

Refreshments will be served

Call _____if you have not confirmed your families' attendance.

Content Areas

Art
Literacy
Math
Problem Solving

Purpose

To learn how daily activities at home and at school can help children to develop positive attitudes about math.

Related Books

Five Creatures by Emily Jenkins
Millions of Cats by Wanda Gag
Eating Fractions by Bruce McMillan

Nametags

Materials

Pattern for making eye nametag (see next page)
Colored construction paper (yellow, red, blue, green, orange, tan)
Markers
Scissors

- Use the eye pattern (see next page) to make nametags in six colors.
- Assign one color per family.
- Different colored nametags will be used to assign families to one of six activity stations.
- Make an extra set of nametags in each of the six colors to post at the activity stations.
- Give each family member the same color nametag to enable them to rotate through the six stations together.

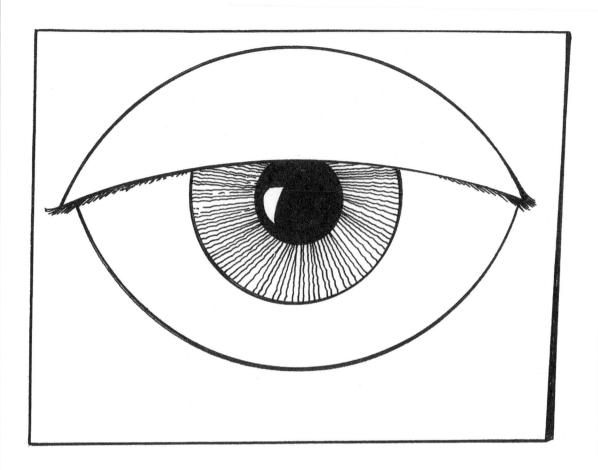

Mixer—What's Your Estimation? or Is That Your Final Answer?

- As families arrive, distribute the nametags.
- Ask family members to write their names on the nametags and use masking tape to attach them to their clothing.
- Be sure all members of each family have the same color nametag so they can work together at each activity station.
- Ask everyone to sit in chairs arranged in a large circle in the center of the room.
- Stand in the center of the circle, holding a baby food jar filled with colored jellybeans.
- Give each family a few moments to collaborate as they try to guess how many beans are in the jar.
- Ask one person from each household to introduce their family members and give their estimation of the number of beans in the jar.
- The family that gives the correct or closest answer gets to keep the candy.

Introduction

Children learn positive attitudes about mathematics by doing activities that are a part of daily life and of interest to them. Help children seek solutions to concrete problems, such as constructing with blocks; measuring sand, water, or ingredients for cooking; observing and recording changes in the environment; and classifying everyday objects. Opportunities to learn mathematical concepts abound in everyday life. The activities in this family meeting emphasize fun, learning, and things that they can do with their children at home.

Tell the families to look at the color on their nametags. Each family starts at the activity station that is the same color. When they notice the lights flickering, that is the signal to move clockwise to the next activity station. The four activity stations are:

1. Shoebox Button Toss (blue)
2. My Number Book (green)
3. Number Fun Bingo (orange)
4. Snack Time Math (red)

Family Meeting Activities

Station #1: Shoebox Button Toss

(blue #1 nametag)

This activity develops both number recognition and motor skills.

Materials

10 adult size shoeboxes with lids
Markers
55 plastic or metal buttons
Index cards or tagboard cut into cards 2" x 2"
Masking tape
Cloth bag with drawstring

What to Do

Before the family meeting, use a marker to number each box lid with numerals and corresponding dots 1 through 10. Place the 10 open shoeboxes in a row against a wall about two feet apart. Place the numbered shoebox lids directly behind the shoeboxes. Draw numbers from 1 to 10 on an appropriate number of index cards. Put the cards in a cloth bag. Mark a line with masking tape to designate where the players will stand as they toss the buttons. This line can be adjusted to a closer or farther distance depending on the age of the player.

1. Reach into a closed bag and draw a card marked with a number represented by dots as well as the numeral. This card indicates which box to toss your buttons into.
2. In turn, toss buttons into the correct shoebox until the amount of buttons in the box corresponds to the number on the shoebox lid.
3. The other participants count aloud as each of the buttons are tossed.
4. Continue until all numbers have been drawn.

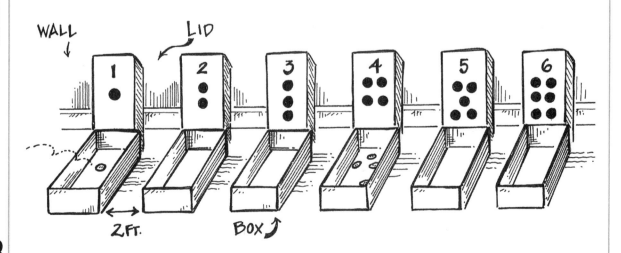

WALL
LID
2 FT.
BOX

Station #2: My Number Book

(green #2 nametag)

This activity reinforces number correspondence and literacy skills.

Materials

8 ½" x 11" letter size unlined paper
Stapler
Hole punch
Colored yarn
Scissors
Markers or crayons
Variety of picture catalogs and magazines
Glue or paste

What to Do

1. Take six sheets of unlined paper. Align each sheet of paper and fold it in half.
2. Staple the pages together.
3. On the cover, print the title "My Number Book, by (child's name)."
4. Using markers or crayons, write numerals with corresponding dots on each page, 1 through 10.
5. Cut out small pictures from catalogues.
6. Paste one picture on page one, two pictures on page two, three pictures on page three, and so on.
7. Continue until completed. If you run out of time, complete the book at home.

6 SHEETS of UNLINED PAPER

11"

8½"

ALIGN SHEETS and FOLD IN HALF

MY NUMBER Book by ELLIE

TITLE of BOOK and CHILD'S NAME

Station #3: Number Fun Bingo

(orange #3 nametag)

This activity reinforces number recognition.

Materials
Poster board bingo cards (see example below)
Markers
Bingo chips
Index cards
Bag or box

What to Do
Before the meeting, make bingo cards with three columns and three rows. Print an assortment of the numerals from 1-10 in different order on each of the cards. The center square will be free. Print the numeral from 1-10 on the index cards.

1. The group chooses a caller.
2. The rest of the participants select a bingo number card. Play as a family team or individually.
3. The caller reaches into the bag and calls out the number on the card.
4. The rest of the partici-pants place real bingo chips in the correct columns as numbers are called.
5. Continue play until everyone gets a row of number bingo, or play until all spaces are filled.

4	1	7
6	FREE	3
2	8	5

MEANINGFUL MATH

Station #4: Snack Time Math

(red #4 nametag)

Create nutritious snacks with this activity, and learn counting and measurement skills.

Materials
Paper bowls for each participant
Teaspoon measuring spoons
Raisins
Peanuts
Sunflower seeds
Coconut flakes
Chocolate or carob chips (optional)
Plastic spoons

What to Do
1. Put 2 teaspoons of raisins in a bowl.
2. Add 1 teaspoon of peanuts.
3. Add 1 teaspoon of sunflower seeds.
4. Add 1 teaspoon of coconut.
5. If desired, add 1 teaspoon of chocolate or carob chips.
6. Mix ingredients together in bowl.
7. Eat now!

Note: Check to be sure there are no food allergies in the group.

Thank everyone for coming and ask participants to fill out the evaluation forms. Invite them to share a snack of juice and crackers.

EVALUATION

Meaningful Math

Family Meeting Evaluation

How did we do?

Please color in the bear's hat that best describes how your family felt about this workshop.

"Hats off!"   "Just a tip of the hat."   "Hats on."

Comments and Suggestions

_____

_____

_____

_____

_____

_____

_____

_____

Thank you for coming!

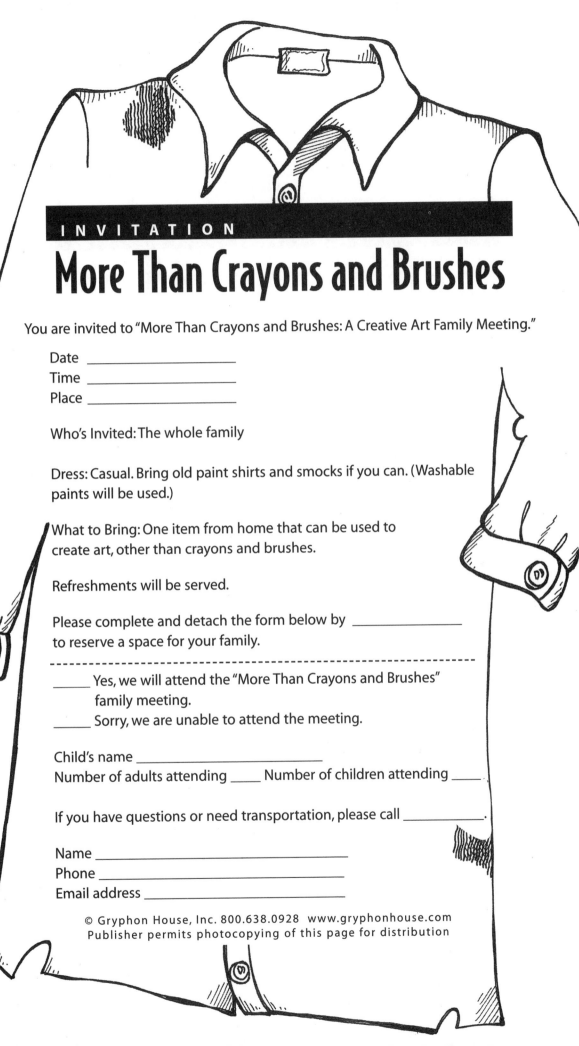

More Than Crayons and Brushes

You are invited to "More Than Crayons and Brushes: A Creative Art Family Meeting."

Date _____

Time _____

Place _____

Who's Invited: The whole family

Dress: Casual. Bring old paint shirts and smocks if you can. (Washable paints will be used.)

What to Bring: One item from home that can be used to create art, other than crayons and brushes.

Refreshments will be served.

Please complete and detach the form below by _____ to reserve a space for your family.

- -

_____ Yes, we will attend the "More Than Crayons and Brushes" family meeting.

_____ Sorry, we are unable to attend the meeting.

Child's name _____

Number of adults attending _____ Number of children attending _____

If you have questions or need transportation, please call _____.

Name _____

Phone _____

Email address _____

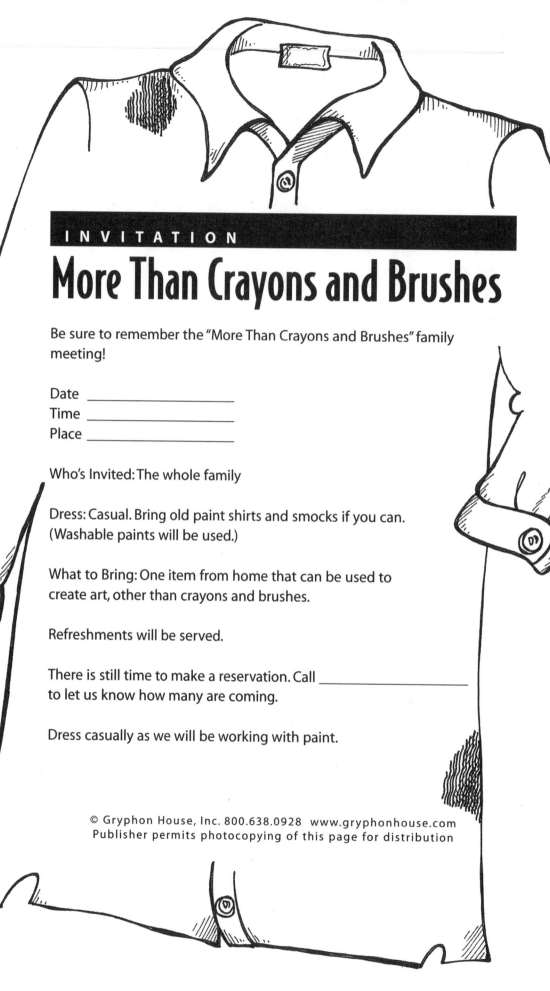

More Than Crayons and Brushes

Be sure to remember the "More Than Crayons and Brushes" family meeting!

Date _____

Time _____

Place _____

Who's Invited: The whole family

Dress: Casual. Bring old paint shirts and smocks if you can. (Washable paints will be used.)

What to Bring: One item from home that can be used to create art, other than crayons and brushes.

Refreshments will be served.

There is still time to make a reservation. Call _____ to let us know how many are coming.

Dress casually as we will be working with paint.

Content Areas
Art
Motor Skills
Problem Solving

Purpose
To provide families with an opportunity to create artwork with tools other than paintbrushes and crayons.

Related Book
Harold and the Purple Crayon by Crockett Johnson

Nametags

Materials
Construction paper or tagboard
Shirt pattern (at right)
Scissors
Markers
Masking tape

- Use the shirt pattern (at right) to make nametags.
- Write 1, 2, 3, 4, or 5 on the lower right corner of each nametag. Assign one number per family.
- The nametags will be used to assign families to one of five activity stations.
- Make an extra set of nametags to post at the activity stations.

Mixer

- As families arrive, distribute the nametags.
- Ask each family member to write his or her name on the nametag and use masking tape to attach it to his or her clothing.
- Be sure all members of each family have the same number on their nametags so they can work together at each activity station.
- As all the families arrive, form a large circle.
- Each family will select someone to introduce themselves and their other family members.
- This person will also show the item their family brought from home to do creative painting.

Introduction

The activities in this family meeting use unusual materials to create artwork. "The purpose of art in the early childhood curriculum is to allow children to explore artistic media and to provide a vehicle for the creative expression of each child. Art is not the work of others (teachers' or parents' models), nor is it coloring inside lines of a drawing. It is a process not a product. It is often messy and incomplete by our adult standards, but it is a representation of the child's work as he/she can express it" (Schiller and Rossano, *The Instant Curriculum*, 1990).

Tell families they should go to the station that has the same number as the one on their nametags. They should work together at that station until they hear a signal (a bell, a whistle, or any other signal) to clean up the activity station and move clockwise to the next station. The activity stations for this meeting are:

1. Tennis Ball Roll Art
2. Feather Painting
3. Object Prints
4. Magical Magnet Masterpieces
5. Color Blowing

Note: The art masterpieces created during this family meeting will be saved and sent home when they are dry. Be sure to sign each one.

Family Meeting Activities

Station #1: Tennis Ball Roll Art
(#1 nametag)

A cooperative color creation that is sure to delight everyone.

Materials
Empty sand and water table
Newspaper
Tennis balls
Several squeeze bottles containing a variety of colored liquid
   tempera paint
Newsprint
Paper towels and water for cleanup

What to Do
1. Line the sand and water table with newspaper.
2. Squeeze or pour about ¼ cup of a variety of colors of liquid tempera onto the paper. Keep the colors separate.
3. Put a piece of newsprint in the sand and water table.
3. Place four tennis balls on the table.
4. Families in the group surround the table and tip it from side to side to initiate and continue the rolling of the balls. Note the variety of colored lines that form as the tennis balls roll.
5. When finished, remove the newsprint and let it dry.
6. Remove the tennis balls, roll up the newspaper, and clean hands.

Station #2: Feather Painting

(#2 nametag)

Feathers make unique painting tools that produce effects far different from any other type of brush.

Materials

Paper
Variety of feathers both large and small
Liquid tempera in a variety of colors
Paper bowls or plastic margarine tubs to serve as paint containers
Paper towels and water for cleanup

What to Do

Prior to the family meeting, pour a small amount of each color of tempera paint into a plastic bowl or margarine tub.

1. Dip feathers into tempera.
2. Apply the paint to the paper using a variety of feather sizes.
3. Use both ends of feather, if desired.

Station #3: Object Prints

(#3 nametag)

Discover that object printing is a simple method of transferring a design from the surface of one object to some other surface.

Materials

Paper
Small wood blocks, jar lids, sponges, cookie cutters, Q tips, or other objects
Liquid tempera (choose colors that will contrast with the shade of
    paper used)
Shallow containers or dishes
Paper towels and water for cleanup

What to Do

Prior to the meeting, pour small amounts of a variety of colors of liquid tempera into the shallow containers.

1. Dip objects into the paint.
2. Press objects on the paper to transfer the print design.

Station #4: Magical Magnet Masterpieces

(#4 nametag)

(Adapted from *Mudpies to Magnets* by Williams, Rockwell, Sherwood)

Discover how to use magnets to create a unique art masterpiece.

Materials
Paper plates
Small metal objects, such as paper clips, nails, or washers
Liquid tempera paint (blue, red, and yellow)
Magnets (wand magnets work well, especially with the paper plates)

What to Do
1. Pour several drops of each color of paint on the plate.
2. Place metal objects on the plate.
3. Help your child hold the magnet against the bottom of the plate and move it in a circular fashion.
4. As the magnet attracts the metal objects, the paint will create a design.

Note: Cake pans with paper cut to fit into them work well and prevent spilling. The advantage of the paper plates is that they are lightweight and easy to handle.

Station #5: Color Blowing

(#5 nametag)

Learn about air movement by blowing paint around the surface of a piece of paper.

Materials
Large straws   Smooth paper
Liquid tempera   Containers for paint
Plastic spoons

What to Do
Before the meeting, pour a few colors of liquid tempera paint into separate containers. Thin with a bit of water.
1. Use a spoon to put a few drops of tempera paint on the paper.
2. Hold the straw as close as you can and blow the paint over the surface of the paper.

Thank everyone for coming and invite them to share a snack of seasonal fruit and crackers after completing the evaluation form.

EVALUATION

More Than Crayons and Brushes

Family Meeting Evaluation

Please circle the hand that best describes your opinion of this workshop. Your thoughts and comments are important to us.

Comments and Suggestions

_____

_____

_____

_____

_____

_____

_____

_____

_____

_____

Thank you for coming!

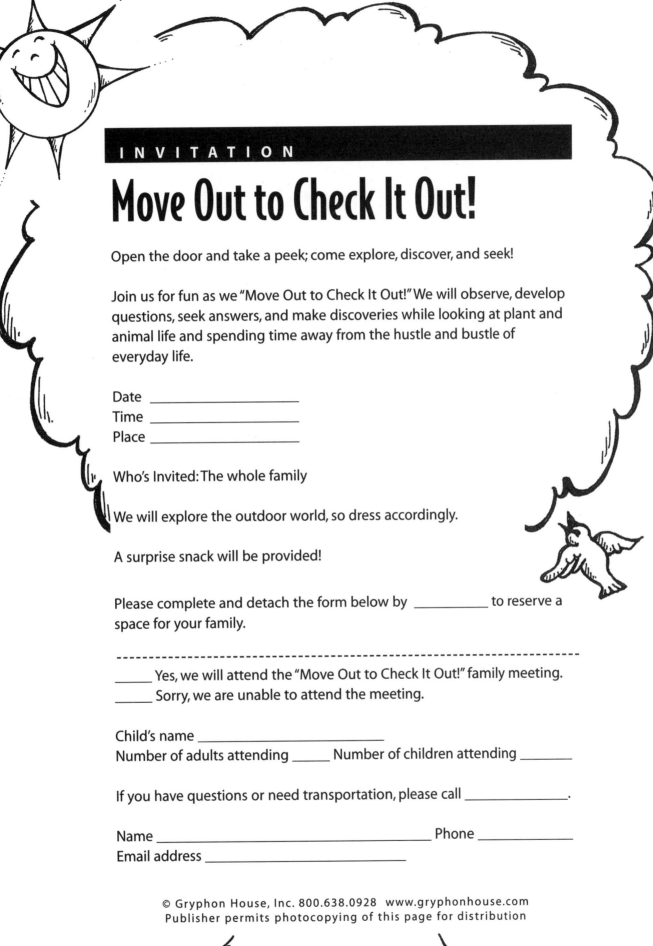

Move Out to Check It Out!

Open the door and take a peek; come explore, discover, and seek!

Join us for fun as we "Move Out to Check It Out!" We will observe, develop questions, seek answers, and make discoveries while looking at plant and animal life and spending time away from the hustle and bustle of everyday life.

Date _____
Time _____
Place _____

Who's Invited: The whole family

We will explore the outdoor world, so dress accordingly.

A surprise snack will be provided!

Please complete and detach the form below by _____ to reserve a space for your family.

_____ Yes, we will attend the "Move Out to Check It Out!" family meeting.
_____ Sorry, we are unable to attend the meeting.

Child's name _____
Number of adults attending _____ Number of children attending _____

If you have questions or need transportation, please call _____.

Name _____ Phone _____
Email address _____

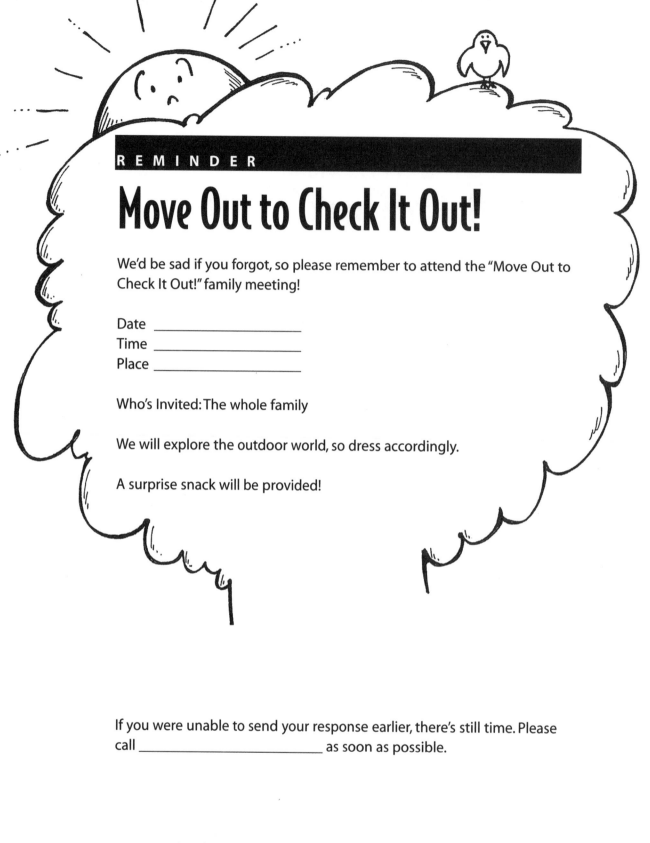

Move Out to Check It Out!

We'd be sad if you forgot, so please remember to attend the "Move Out to Check It Out!" family meeting!

Date _____

Time _____

Place _____

Who's Invited: The whole family

We will explore the outdoor world, so dress accordingly.

A surprise snack will be provided!

If you were unable to send your response earlier, there's still time. Please call _____ as soon as possible.

Content Areas
Art
Problem Solving
Science
Social Development

Purpose
To observe, develop questions, seek answers, and make discoveries while looking at plant and animal life and spending time away from the hustle and bustle of everyday life.
Note: This family meeting works best in warm weather during daylight hours.

Related Books
Fall Is Not Easy by Marty Kelley
In the Small, Small Pond by Denise Fleming
In the Tall, Tall Grass by Denise Fleming
Ugh! A Bug by Mary Bono
Where Does the Butterfly Go When It Rains? by May Garelick

Nametags

Materials
Red, yellow, green, and orange construction paper
Scissors
Patterns (see next page)
Markers

- Use the patterns (see next page) to make nametags in four shapes. Use a different color construction paper for each shape, such as a green tree, a yellow sun, red flower, and an orange insect.
- Assign one shape per family.
- Different colored nametags will be used to assign families to one of four activity stations.
- Make an extra set of nametags in each of the four shapes to post at the activity stations.

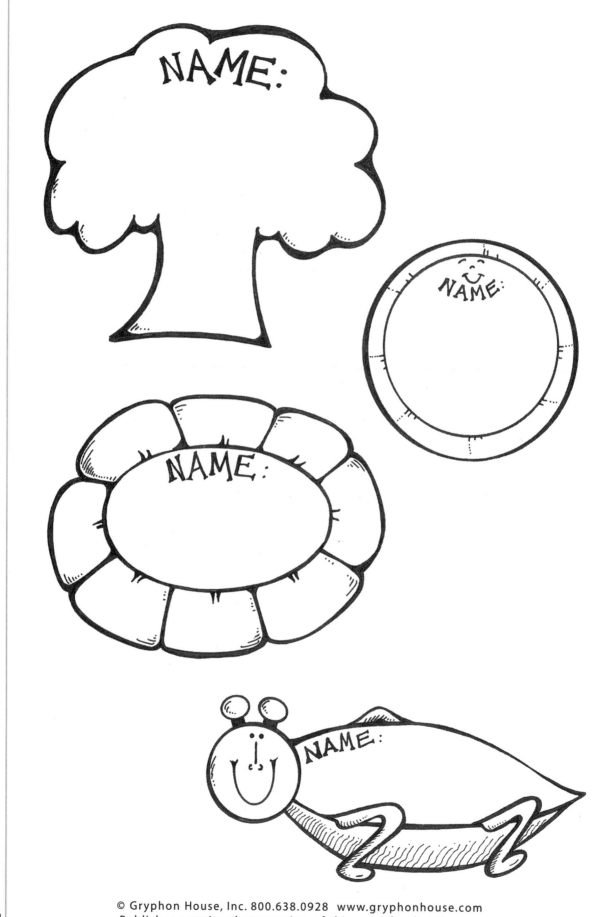

Move Out to Check It Out!

Mixer

- As families arrive, distribute the nametags.
- Ask each family member to write his or her name on the nametag and use masking tape to attach it to his or her clothing.
- Be sure all members of each family have the same shape nametag so they will work together at each activity station.
- Give each family a copy of the "Friends of Nature" Scavenger Hunt (page 221) and a pencil as they arrive. Explain that when they find someone who fits the description on the sheet, they should write the person's name on the line provided.
- Reassemble the group after approximately five to ten minutes.
- Ask if anyone was able to complete the entire scavenger hunt or if anyone learned something interesting about a person they met.

Introduction

This family meeting will provide an opportunity to explore and discover our outdoor world by turning our attention to nature to understand and appreciate our environment. The outdoors will turn into our science lab as we observe, discover, and create.

Tell the families to begin at the activity station designated by the symbol on their nametags. If the nametag is a sun, begin at the sun station. If it is a tree, begin at the tree station, and so on. When families hear a whistle, that is the signal to rotate to the next station. The first whistle is a reminder to finish the activity and straighten the station, if necessary. The second whistle is the signal to move clockwise to the next station. The four activity stations are:

1. Camouflage Hide-and-Seek (orange insect)
2. Sensational Seed Search (green tree)
3. Happy Habitats (yellow sun)
4. Nature Bookmarks (red flower)

Family Meeting Activities

Station #1: Camouflage Hide-and-Seek

(insect nametag)

Materials

Variety of colored construction paper circles, approximately 1 $\frac{1}{2}$" in green, brown, gray, red, yellow, and blue

Pictures of insects and animals showing their camouflage (*Big Backyard* and *Ranger Rick* magazines are excellent sources)

Who's Hiding Here? by Yoshi

What to Do

Before the meeting, collect and laminate pictures of insect and animals showing how they use their natural camouflage to blend into their surroundings.

1. As a group, talk about what camouflage means and how and why insects and animals "hide" from other animals.
2. Choose one person from the group to read *Who's Hiding Here?*
3. After listening to the story, one member of each family takes one color of construction paper circles. (The circles represent insects.)
4. Find different places the "insects" could blend into their surroundings. For example, the green circle will blend in with grass or leaves. The gray circles will blend in with tree bark.
5. After a few minutes, discuss the different hiding places you found for the "insects."

Station #2: Sensational Seed Search

(green tree nametag)

Explore and discover seeds found in nature by collecting and attempting to germinate the seeds.

Materials

Zipper-closure plastic bags (quart size)

Magnifying glasses or other hand lenses (optional)

Paper towels

Bucket of water

What to Do

1. Take a short walk around the building. Look for seeds found in nature, such as dandelion seeds, acorns, or maple tree seeds. As you find seeds,

216

place them in a zipper-closure plastic bag.

2. After the walk, share what you found with the members of the group. If possible, use hand lenses to examine the seeds. Discuss how seeds grow into plants or trees. Predict whether any of their seeds will grow into plants.

3. Help children wet a paper towel by dipping it in the bucket of water and squeezing out any excess water.

4. Help them fold the paper towel carefully so it will fit inside the zipper-closure plastic bag.

5. Before placing the moist paper towel in the zipper-closure plastic bag, lay the seeds on the paper towel.

6. Place the seeds and the paper towel in the zipper-closure plastic bag and seal it.

7. Take your seed bags home and check them every few days to see if there are any changes.

Station #3: Happy Habitats
(yellow sun nametag)

Develop a new awareness of the variety of plant and animal life and record the findings.

Materials
Wire hangers shaped into circles (one per family)
Clipboard (made from piece of cardboard with paper clips holding paper in place)
Pencils

What to Do
Before the meeting, shape wire hangers into circles.

1. Find a spot in the grass to place your circle-shaped hanger. The area within your hanger is the habitat you will study.

2. Observe the area within your hanger for five to ten minutes. Observe the ground, as well as the area directly above your hanger.

3. As a family, record what you see on your paper. Use words and pictures while recording. Include animal life, as well as plant life. Since the area directly above your hanger is included, birds flying above the hanger are included.

4. When the observation time is up, share what you saw in the habitats.

Station #4: Nature Bookmarks
(red flower nametag)

Preserve a nature treasure with this make-it-and-take-it project.

Materials
2" x 5" tagboard, 1 per person
2" x 5" sheets of clear contact paper, 2 per person
Hole punch
Ribbon or yarn
A variety of small flowers or petals, leaves, and clovers
Markers
Scissors

What to Do
Because this activity requires trimming and assembly, it is helpful to provide a working area such as a table.

1. Get a piece of tagboard and two pieces of contact paper. Write your name on the tagboard. (Help your child write his or her name, if necessary.)
2. Remove the backing from a piece of contact paper and arrange the flowers or leaves on the sticky side of the contact paper.
3. Stick the contact paper with the arranged flowers or leaves onto the tagboard. Trim off any edges that hang over.
4. Remove the backing from the second piece of contact paper. Place it on the other side of the tagboard and trim away any edges that extend over the tagboard.
5. Punch a hole at the top of the bookmark. Tie a piece of ribbon or yarn through the hole.

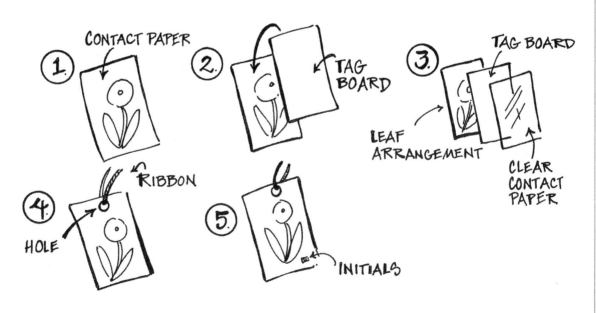

Group Activity—Snack: Dirt Desserts

Materials

8 oz. clear plastic cups, 1 per person
Chocolate pudding
Crushed chocolate wafer cookies
Gummy worms
$\frac{1}{2}$ cup measuring cup
1 tablespoon for measuring sprinkles
Plastic spoons, 1 per person

What to Do

If possible, before the meeting make chocolate pudding with the children. If not, bring prepared chocolate pudding to the meeting. Depending on the number of people attending the meeting, it may be necessary to set up two or three snack stations so families don't have to wait too long to make their snack.

1. Fill the measuring cup with chocolate pudding.
2. Pour the chocolate pudding into the clear plastic cup.
3. Sprinkle 1 tablespoon of chocolate sprinkles on top of the pudding.
4. Add 1 to 2 gummy worms to each cup.
5. Eat the yummy dirt desserts!

Note: As with any activity involving food, be aware of food allergies and/or preferences.

Thank everyone for coming and ask them to fill out an evaluation form before they leave.

EVALUATION

Move Out to Check It Out!

Family Meeting Evaluation

Please let us know what you thought of today's meeting. Your thoughts and comments are important to us. Thank you.

Sunny
(great meeting)

Cloudy
(OK meeting)

Rainy
(not much of a meeting)

Comments and Suggestions

_____

_____

_____

_____

_____

_____

_____

Thank you for coming!

Friends of Nature Scavenger Hunt

When you find someone who fits the description on the sheet, ask them to sign their name on the line provided.

Find someone who...

1. Has camped out in the last month. _____

2. Has planted a tree recently. _____

3. Has a vegetable garden. _____

4. Has done something to help clean our environment. _____

5. Likes to go apple picking. _____

6. Enjoys hiking. _____

7. Has a bug collection. _____

8. Collects four-leaf clovers. _____

9. Has a flower garden. _____

10. Has a leaf collection. _____

11. Collects bird nests. _____

12. Enjoys fishing. _____

Number Fun Family Night

Dear Family,
Come and learn fun things you can do at home to help your child recognize and know numerals 1 through 10. You can participate in all of the activities with your children. By the end of the meeting, you will know some useful and fun ideas to try at home.

Date _____

Time _____

Place _____

Who's Invited: The whole family

We want you to be comfortable, so please dress casually. The meeting will last about 1 ½ hours and will start and finish on time. We will also have refreshments.

We look forward to seeing everyone for a night of number fun.

Please complete and detach the form below by _____ to reserve a space for your family.

_____ Yes, we will attend the "Number Fun Family Night" family meeting.
_____ Sorry, we are unable to attend the meeting.

Child's name _____

Number of adults attending _____ Number of children attending _____

If you have questions or need transportation, please call _____.

Name _____ Phone _____

Email address _____

Number Fun Family Night

Don't forget!

Your family is invited to a "Number Fun Family Night."

Date _____

Time _____

Place _____

Who's Invited: The whole family

Dress: Casual

Please reserve an hour and a half to participate in fun math activities that are designed to teach and reinforce beginning number recognition with your child.

If you haven't made your reservation there is still time. Please call _____ to RSVP.

See you on the _____.

Content Area
Mathematics

Purpose
To provide families with activities they can do at home to develop number recognition.

Related Books
Let's Count by Tana Hoban
Low Song by Eve Merriam
One, Two, Skip a Few by Roberta Arenson

Nametags

Materials
Playing cards with the numeral nine or lower
Masking tape
Marker

- Place a piece of masking tape on the bottom of the front of each playing card.
- Also place a piece of masking tape on the lower right corner of the back of each playing card. Put the numeral 1, 2, 3, 4, or 5 on the masking tape. Assign one of these five numbers per family.
- Numbers on the backs of the playing cards will be used to assign families to one of four activity stations.

Mixer—What's My Number?

- As families arrive, distribute the nametags.
- Ask each family member to write his or her name on the piece of masking tape on the front of the card and use masking tape to attach it to his or her clothing.
- Be sure all members of each family have a nametag with the same number on the back so they will work together at each activity station.
- Ask the participants to check and remember the number on the back of their nametag before the mixer begins.

- Divide the participants into two groups. Half of the group stands and forms a circle facing outward. The rest stands and forms a circle around the first group so they are facing someone in the inner circle.
- Give a starting signal (a ringing bell) and ask the inside group to move counterclockwise, while the outer group moves clockwise. Ring the bell again and everyone stops.
- The participants facing each other begin by stating their first name and asking, "What's my number?" The person they are facing guesses a number. If the guess matches the number on the back of their nametag, the response is, "Correct." If not, the answer is "Try again." Each participant is given two guesses.
- Repeat, allowing 10 minutes for this activity. By then, all or most of the participants will have met each other.

Introduction

This family meeting has activities that show how to help preschool children recognize and understand simple numbers, and become familiar with number names. Young children may know the numbers in their address or the number that represents their age, but they still have a limited understanding of numbers. Their familiarity of numbers can be increased through number rhymes and songs or stories that utilize numbers. Some examples are the rhyme "Three Blind Mice" or the story of *The Three Bears*. Children also hear and use numbers when they play games.

Tell the families to move to the activity station that matches the numeral on the back lower right side of their nametags. They will rotate clockwise when they hear a signal, such as "One Potato, Two Potato," "One, Two, Buckle My Shoe," or "Five Little Ducks." The five activity stations are:

1. Number Rummy
2. Number Concentration
3. Number Jewelry
4. Musical Numbers
5. Number Race

Family Meeting Activities

Station #1: Number Rummy

(#1 nametag)

Materials
Tagboard and scissors, or index cards
Markers

What to Do
Before the meeting, prepare a deck of 52 tagboard (or index) cards. Twenty-six cards will contain numerals 1 through 10 and twenty-six will have drawings or stickers of the corresponding numbers. If the group is large, make more than one deck. Prepare a take-home handout that details how to make the cards.

1. Shuffle the cards and deal five to each player.
2. Place the remaining cards face down in the center of the table. Turn the first card of the deck over to make a discard pile. (The object of the game is to make as many pairs as possible.)
3. Each player takes a turn and draws a card from either the face down or face up deck.
4. The player then either plays a pair or discards one card. (To play a pair, the player places a numeral card face up and a card with the corresponding number of objects face up. Two sets of objects or two sets of numerals do not make a pair.)
5. Play continues until one player has run out of cards.
6. Count each player's pairs to determine the winner.

Station #2: Number Concentration

(#2 nametag)

Materials
Tagboard and scissors, or index cards
Markers

What to Do
Before the meeting prepare a deck of 52 tagboard (or index) cards. Twenty-six cards will contain numerals 1 through 10, and 26 will have drawings or stickers of the corresponding numbers. If the group is large, make more than one deck.

Note: These cards are made the same way as the cards used at activity station #1 for Number Rummy.)

1. Shuffle the cards and arrange them face down in rows.
2. In turn, each player turns over two cards and names the numeral or number of objects on each card.
3. If the two cards match, the player keeps them. If not, the player turns the cards face down and the next player begins play.
4. When all matches are made, the player with the most cards wins.

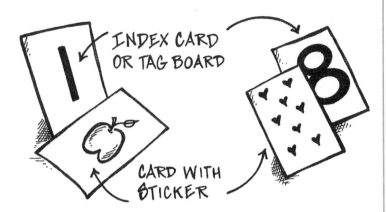

Station #3: Number Jewelry

(#3 nametag)

Materials
Beads
Paper bowls
Lacing string
Number cards made from construction paper or tagboard cut to 2"x 2" in size.
Hole punch

What to Do
1. Each participant takes a lacing string and a number card.
2. Punch a hole in the number card and thread it with the lacing string.
3. String the number card first.
4. String the number of beads that correspond to the number card.
5. Tie the necklace and wear it for the duration of the meeting.

Station #4: Musical Numbers

(#4 nametag)

To associate numerals with the correct number.

Materials
Set of 3 x 5 index cards
10 pieces of 9" x 12" poster board or tag board
Happy face stickers placed on the tag board to match the corresponding
    numbers 1-10
Crayons
Tape recorder or record player
Music

What to Do
Before the meeting, write each of the numerals 1-10 on a separate piece of
poster board or tag board. Put the corresponding number of happy face
stickers on each piece of poster board. Place these pieces of poster board
on the floor in a circle.
1. Each participant takes 10 index cards.
2. Help your child use crayons to write the numerals 1-10 on the cards.
3. Take your set of numbers and stand on an imaginary path just behind
    a tag board number on the floor.
Note: Two circles may be necessary if the group is large.
4. One participant plays the music. When the music starts, walk clockwise
    around the path.
5. When the music stops, hold up the number card that corresponds to
    the number of objects on the poster board you are standing behind.
6. The participant playing the music removes one floor card.
7. Everyone also discards the corresponding number card from those
    they are holding.
8. Music begins again.
9. When the music stops again one player will not be behind a floor card.
    That player is out and helps with the music and collecting the
    discarded cards.
10. Continue playing as time permits.

Station #5: Number Race

(#5 nametag)

To associate numerals with numbers.

Materials
Large number cards 9" x 12" each with 1-10 objects
Two sets of cards numbered 1-10
Masking tape

What to Do
(Before the meeting, use masking tape to mark two starting lines on the floor.)
1. Form two teams. Select one person to hold up the cards.
2. Place one set of number cards a short distance away from both teams, on a shelf or table.
4. A player from each team stands at the starting line.
5. The person selected in step #1 flashes one of the large number cards.
6. The two players from each team run for their number cards. The first one to hold up the correct card wins a point for the team.
7. The team with the most points wins.

Thank everyone for coming and invite them to share a snack of seasonal fruit and crackers after they complete an evaluation form.

EVALUATION

Number Fun Family Night

Family Meeting Evaluation

How did it add up?

GOOD _____   OKAY _____   POOR _____

Comments and Suggestions

_____

_____

_____

_____

_____

_____

_____

_____

_____

_____

_____

Thank you for coming!

Raisin' Your Nutritional IQ

You're invited to learn some fun and simple recipes that you can make with your children!

Date _____

Time _____

Place _____

Who's Invited: The whole family

Dress: Casual

Nutritious snacks will be served during the meeting!

Please complete and detach the form below by _____ to reserve a space for your family.

- -

_____ Yes, we will attend the "Raisin' Your Nutritional IQ" family meeting.

_____ Sorry, we are unable to attend the meeting.

Child's name _____

Number of adults attending _____ Number of children attending _____

If you have questions or need transportation, please call _____.

Name _____ Phone _____

Email address _____

REMINDER

Raisin' Your Nutritional IQ

Don't forget to come to this family meeting!

Date _____

Time _____

Place _____

Who's Invited: The whole family

Dress: Casual

Nutritious snacks will be served during the meeting!

Questions or responses? Call _____.

Content Areas
Language
Math
Motor Skills
Science

Purpose
To understand some of the developmental skills children learn when preparing simple nutritious snacks that can be made at home, and to enhance awareness of nutritious snacks for children.

Food Allergies: Be aware of any food allergies children may have. Some of the more common foods to which children may be allergic are wheat, milk and milk products, juices that have a high acid content such as orange or grapefruit, chocolate, eggs, and nuts. When families call to make reservations, inform them about the foods that will be used at this meeting.

Cultural Factors: The cultural and ethnic customs of our society influence the food we eat. Different ethnic groups in the United States may follow various dietary patterns and food preferences. A family's cultural heritage often determines whether a particular food is eaten, regardless of its nutrient value. Inform families as stated above.

Related Books
I Eat Fruit by Hannah Tofts
I Eat Vegetables by Hannah Tofts
I Will Never Not Ever Eat a Tomato by Lauren Child

Nametags

Materials
Red, yellow, green, and blue construction paper
Scissors
Raisin pattern (see next page)
Markers

- Use the raisin pattern (see next page) to make nametags in four colors.
- Assign one color per family.
- Different-colored nametags will be used to assign families to one of four activity stations.

- Make an extra set of nametags in each of the four colors to post at the activity stations.

Mixer

- As families arrive, distribute the raisin nametags.
- Ask each family member to write his or her name on the nametag and use masking tape to attach it to his or her clothing.
- Be sure all members of each family have the same color nametag so they will work together at each activity station.
- Write the name of one nutritious snack item (see suggestions on the next page) on the back of each family's nametag as they arrive. Tell families to familiarize themselves with their snack item name. Each family can talk about their snack item as they await the start of the meeting. Ask families not to share this snack name with the other families, as they will be playing a guessing game as they get acquainted.
- After all of the families have arrived, ask the families to circulate, introduce themselves, and then ask questions about the other family's snack item until they are able to identify it. For example, if the snack item is an apple, the following are possible apple questions: "Is it red?" Answer: "Sometimes." "Does it have seeds?" "Yes." "Does it grow on a tree?" "Yes." "Is it harvested in the fall?" "Yes." And so on, until they get the correct answer.

- Families reverse roles, and the second family asks the questions.
- Then the first family moves on to another family and repeats the process.

Suggested Nutritious Snack Items:
carrots, celery, apple, pear, grapes, banana, cauliflower, nuts, raisins, strawberries, orange, peach, kiwifruit, cantaloupe, nectarine, apricot, popcorn, pineapple, sunflower seeds, dates, broccoli, peanuts, peanut butter, roasted soybeans, cheese, yogurt, milk

● See food allergy information on page 233.

Introduction

The activities in this family meeting combine food with fun and nutrition. They also encourage the participants to try both a variety of foods and new foods. In addition to making nutritional snacks, the activities also teach math (counting, measuring), motor skills (mixing, stirring, using small muscles), language skills (naming, tasting, expressing likes and dislikes), and science (estimating, predicting, senses, comparisons).

The four nutritional snacks are prepared at each activity station. All families with green nametags will start at station one, white at station two, brown at station three, and yellow at station four. Families will make and eat a nutritious snack at each of the four stations. The signal that it is time to move clockwise to the next activity station is "I Heard It Through the Grapevine." Remind participants that it is extremely important to thoroughly wash and dry their hands prior to starting each station. (Make dry wipes available if there is not a convenient water source.) The four activity stations are:

1. Vegetable Wrap (green nametag)
2. Raisin Bread Shapes (yellow nametag)
3. Applesauce Goodie (red nametag)
4. Ants on a Log (blue nametag)

Note: Provide copies of the four recipes plus three additional ones for participants to take home (pages 240-246). Make these into a recipe book, if desired.

Family Meeting Activities

Station #1: Vegetable Wrap

(green nametag)

Materials

Heads of lettuce torn into single leaves
Variety of salad dressings
Bowls
Plastic spoons
Cubed cucumbers, shredded carrots, and cauliflower separated into
   small pieces
Napkins
Picture recipe (rebus) posted at the station (see page 240)

What to Do

Before the meeting, pour dressings in bowls. Prepare the cucumbers, carrots, and cauliflower.

1. Put 1 spoonful of dressing in the center of one lettuce leaf.
2. Add vegetables as desired, such as cucumbers, shredded carrots, cauliflower, or others.
3. Fold the lettuce and eat!

Station #2: Raisin Bread Shapes

(yellow nametag)

Materials

Plastic knives	Raisin bread
Shaped cookie cutters	Soft cream cheese
Raisins	Sunflower nuts
Small paper plates	Basket for bread scraps
Napkins	

Picture recipe (rebus) posted at at the station (see page 241)

What to Do

1. Take a paper plate and a piece of raisin bread.
2. Choose a cookie cutter, press it into the bread, and use it to cut out the shape. (Place bread scraps into the basket to use for bird food.)
3. Use a plastic knife to spread cream cheese on the shape.
4. Sprinkle with raisins and sunflower seeds, if desired.
5. Cut into rectangles, squares, triangles, or any other shape. Eat!

Station #3: Applesauce Goodie

(red nametag)

Materials

Plastic zipper-closure bags

Small, clear plastic cups (4 oz.)

Tablespoons

Graham crackers

Applesauce

Plastic teaspoons

Napkins

Picture recipe (rebus) posted at the station (see page 243)

What to Do

1. Put a graham cracker in a plastic bag.
2. Seal the zipper lock.
3. Crush the cracker by pressing on the bag with your hands.
4. Put a tablespoon of applesauce in the clear plastic cup and sprinkle a small layer of cracker crumbs on top.
5. Put a second tablespoon of applesauce in the cup and another layer of graham cracker crumbs.
6. Continue layering until the cup is full.
7. Eat and enjoy!

Station #4: Ants on a Log

(blue nametag)

Materials

Clean stalks of celery cut into 4" lengths

Peanut butter or cream cheese

Raisins

Plastic knives

Napkins

Picture recipe (rebus) posted at the station (see page 242)

What to Do

Before the meeting, prepare the celery stalks.

1. Using a knife, spread the peanut butter, cream cheese, or both in a piece of celery.
2. Arrange three or four raisins on top.
3. Eat and enjoy!

Thank everyone for coming and remind them to pick up copies of recipes and fill out an evaluation form before leaving.

EVALUATION

Raisin' Your Nutritional IQ

Family Meeting Evaluation

Did we raise your nutritional IQ?

Please circle the picture that best describes your feelings. We appreciate your feedback, so feel free to make comments. Thank you.

Very much   A little   No way

Comments and Suggestions

_____

_____

_____

_____

_____

_____

_____

Thanks for coming!

Vegetable Wrap

① TAKE 1 lettuce leaf

② PUT 1 spoon of dressing in center of leaf.

③ ADD vegetables like:

- ☑ diced cucumbers
- ☑ shredded carrots
- ☑ cauliflower

...or any others.

④ FOLD lettuce, walk around and eat!

Raisin Bread Shapes

① NEED:

raisin bread

soft cream cheese

② SPREAD
cream cheese on a piece of raisin bread.

③ SPRINKLE with raisins and sunflower seeds.

cream cheese   raisin bread

④ CUT into rectangles, squares, triangles or any other shape you choose.

Ants on a Log

1. NEED:

- Clean stalks of celery cut into 3-5 inch lengths.
- Peanut butter or cream cheese.
- Raisins.

2. SPREAD peanut butter or cream cheese on celery.

3.

PLACE raisins on top to look like ants.

4.

EAT and ENJOY!

  # Applesauce Goodie

① NEED:

-  plastic bag with zip lock
- small paper cup
- tablespoon
- 1 graham cracker
- applesauce
  child's hands

② PUT graham cracker in a plastic bag.

 SEAL BAG

CRUSH crackers with hands.

③ PUT tablespoon of applesauce in the cup

 Sprinkle with layer of crumbs.

④ CONTINUE layering until cup is full.

RAISIN' YOUR NUTRITIONAL IQ

Banana Pudding Shake Up

① NEED:

Baby food jar with lid.

Place 1 tablespoon <u>instant</u> banana pudding mix into jar.

②. ADD:

2 tablespoons of cold milk.

MILK

③. PUT lid on securely and shake for about 45 seconds.

Ready to eat!

④. IF desired, serve with sliced bananas, or add raisins or coconut.

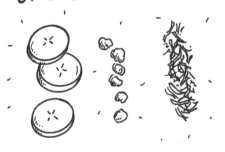

Peanut Butter Balls

① PUT equal amounts of each in a bowl:

- 1 part peanut butter
- 1 part powdered milk
- 1 part honey

② MIX and shape into small balls.

③ WILL be sticky...but fun to make!

Pour crispy rice cereal into another small bowl.

④ ROLL balls in the crispy rice cereal.

Ready to eat!

Raisin Energy Snack

① PUT 2 teaspoons of raisins in a bowl!!

② ADD:
- 1 teaspoon of peanuts
- 1 teaspoon sunflower seeds
- 1 teaspoon coconut
- 1 teaspoon carob chips

③. MIX

④. EAT NOW! Really good for picnics and snacks.

INVITATION

Scientific Art

Dear Families,

As part of our science curriculum, we are involving the children in activities that explore color. Join us as we investigate, explore, and discover how science experiments can be used to create art.

Date _____

Time _____

Place _____

Who's Invited: The whole family

Dress: Casual. Bring an old long-sleeved shirt.

All materials as well as refreshments will be provided.

Please complete and detach the form below by _____ to reserve a space for your family.

_____ Yes, we will attend the "Scientific Art" family meeting.
_____ Sorry, we are unable to attend the meeting.

Child's name _____

Number of adults attending _____ Number of children attending _____

If you have questions or need transportation, please call _____.

Name _____ Phone _____
Email address _____

REMINDER

Scientific Art

Don't forget!

Explore and discover the world of color!

Date _____

Time _____

Place _____

Who's Invited: The whole family

Dress: Casual. Bring an old long-sleeved shirt.

All materials as well as refreshments will be provided.

Come for an evening of science fun!

Please call _____ to RSVP as soon as possible.

Content Areas
Art
Motor Skills
Science

Purpose
To introduce families to science activities that explore the world of color.

Related Books
Brown Bear, Brown Bear, What Do You See? by Bill Martin, Jr. and Eric Carle
Freight Train by Donald Crews
Go Away, Big Green Monster! by Ed Emberly
Little Blue and Little Yellow by Leo Lionni

Nametags

Materials
Red, yellow, green, and blue construction paper
Scissors
Pattern of a maple leaf (see below)
Markers

- Use the maple leaf pattern (at right) to make nametags in four colors.
- Assign one color per family.
- The different colored nametags will be used to assign families to one of four activity stations.
- Make an extra set of nametags in each of the four colors to post at the activity stations.

SCIENTIFIC ART

Mixer

- As families arrive, distribute the maple leaf nametags.
- Ask each family member to write his or her name on a maple leaf and use masking tape to attach it to his or her clothing.
- Be sure all members of each family have the same color nametag so they will work together at each activity station.
- Ask all the participants to stand in a circle.
- Give the ball of yarn to one person. That person introduces his or her family members and shares one activity that the family enjoys doing together.
- That person holds onto the end of the yarn ball and tosses the ball to another person in the circle.
- The person that catches the ball of yarn introduces his or her family and describes one activity the family enjoys doing together. That person also holds onto the yarn and then tosses the ball of yarn to another family.
- Continue until each family has had a turn. After all the families have been introduced, a web will be created. Explain that this web is symbolic of a mixture of the partnership that can arise when many come together to work. This collaborative environment works well at home and in school.

Introduction

The five science activities in this family meeting involve the exploration of color. They use inexpensive materials easily found at home, so families can repeat these activities at home. This will give children an opportunity to work with the materials several times and to refine their skills and knowledge. Children will learn that practice brings improvement and satisfaction.

Ask the families to go to the activity station that is the same color of their nametag. The four activity stations are:

1. Pound a Color (red nametag)
2. Chromatography Butterflies (yellow nametag)
3. Magnet Art (green nametag)
4. Egg Carton Chemistry (blue nametag)

Ask families to listen for a bell ringing, which is the signal that they should clean up the activity station and move clockwise to the next activity station.

Family Meeting Activities

Station #1: Pound a Color

(red nametag)

Plant hammering reveals colors that come from chemicals. These are called pigments. Hammering crushes a leaf or a flower, revealing its structure and creating a pretty print. Do this activity outdoors, or inside on the floor with a rug underneath to absorb the hammering noise.

Materials

Wooden boards 12" x 12" x 1" (enough to accommodate the number of
    families at the station)
White fabric (old sheets) torn into pieces that fit on the wooden boards
Leaves and flowers collected the day of the meeting
Hammers (with adult supervision only)
Safety glasses

What to Do

Before the meeting, collect leaves and flowers.

1. Each family places an arrangement of flowers and leaves on the
    wooden board.
2. Cover the arrangement with the white fabric.
3. Everyone puts on a pair of safety glasses, and hammers all around the
    board, crushing the leaves and flowers so the color is driven into the
    fabric.

Caution: Supervise your child's use of the hammer at all times.

4. Remove the fabric and allow to dry.
5. When the fabric is dry, use your hand to remove crushed plant particles
    gently.
6. Take your print home and frame it as a remembrance of the meeting.

Station #2: Chromatography Butterflies

(yellow nametag)

Chromatography is a process that separates a mixed color into its individual parts. Chemicals in markers are called pigments, which can be separated by adding water.

Materials
Water
Coffee filters
Colored water-soluble markers
Spring type clothespins
Eyedroppers or pipettes

What to Do
1. Use markers to make designs on the coffee filter.
2. Fill eyedroppers with water.
3. Release small drops of water on the coffee filter. Help your child with this step, if necessary.
4. Observe as the color designs defuse to make a rainbow of colors. (See if you can tell which markers use multiple pigments. Black markers use many.)
5. When the filters are dry, have your child twist them to make butterfly wings and place them on a spring-type clothespin to create a pretty butterfly.

Note: Filters will need time to dry. The children can bring home the finished butterflies the next day.

Station #3: Magnet Art

(green nametag)

Metal is attracted by a magnetic force. Add paint to create an artistic masterpiece.

Materials
Shoebox lids
Magnets
White paper
Scissors
Tempera paint (red, yellow, and blue)
Bowls
Spoons
Assortment of small metal objects that are attracted by magnets, such as paper clips, washers, or nails

What to Do

Before the meeting, precut pieces of paper to fit the inside of the shoebox lids. Pour red, yellow, and blue tempera paint into separate bowls. Put a spoon in each bowl.

1. Take a piece of precut paper
2. Place it in a box lid.
3. Put several drops of each color of paint on the paper.
4. Put an assortment of metal objects on the paper.
5. Help your child slide the magnet over the bottom of the box and observe the colors of your artistic creation.
6. Carefully remove the metal objects and then your artwork. Allow to dry.

Station #4: Egg Carton Chemistry

(blue nametag)

Red, yellow, and blue are primary colors. Mix two of these colors together to make a secondary color.

Materials

White Styrofoam egg cartons with tops removed
Eyedroppers or pipettes
Red, yellow, and blue food coloring
Water

What to Do

1. Each family takes an egg carton and an eyedropper or pipette.
2. Fill each section of the egg carton with water.
3. Use the food coloring to make one compartment red, one yellow, and one blue. The remaining nine compartments should contain clear water.
4. Use the eyedroppers or pipettes to create more colors.
5. How many colors can you make?

Thank everyone for coming and invite them to share a snack of seasonal fruit and crackers after completing an evaluation form.

Scientific Art

Family Meeting Evaluation

Please color the thermometer with a crayon to show whether the meeting was hot (good) or cold (poor).

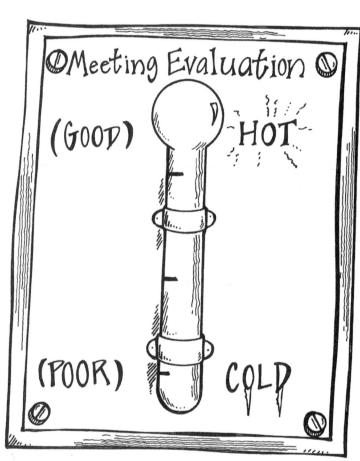

Comments and Suggestions

_____

_____

_____

_____

_____

Thank you for coming!

INVITATION

Shadow Play

Follow me to the "Shadow Play" family meeting.

Date _____
Time _____
Place _____

Who's Invited: The whole family

Dress for fun!

Don't miss this opportunity to have fun making and playing with shadows! You and your children can experience the scientific phenomenon of light exploration and discover the delight of shadow play.

Refreshments will be served.

Please complete and detach the form below by _____ so we can reserve a space for your family.

_____ Yes, we will attend the "Shadow Play" family meeting.
_____ Sorry, we will be unable to attend the meeting.

Child's name _____
Number of adults attending _____ Number of children attending _____

If you have any questions or need transportation, please call _____.

Name _____ Phone _____

Email address _____

REMINDER

Shadow Play

Please remember the "Shadow Play" family meeting.

Date _____

Time _____

Place _____

Who's Invited: The whole family

Dress for fun!

Don't miss this opportunity to have fun making and playing with shadows and discover the delightful wonders of shadow play!

Refreshments will be served.

Content Areas
Dramatic Play
Problem Solving
Science

Purpose
To give participants an opportunity to experience the scientific phenomenon of light exploration, and have fun as they create and discover the delightful wonders of shadow play.

Related Books
Guess Whose Shadow? by Stephen R. Swinburne
Mother, Mother I Feel Sick, Send for the Doctor, Quick Quick Quick by
  Remy Charlip
"My Shadow" from *A Child's Garden of Verses* by Robert Louis Stevenson

Nametags

Materials
Black construction paper
Pen with white ink or white marker
Scissors
Patterns for nametags (see next page)

- Use the patterns (see next page) to cut out five silhouettes from black construction paper, such as a face, an animal, a lunchbox, a gym shoe, and a house.
- Assign one shape per family.
- The different shapes of nametags will be used to assign families to one of five activity stations.
- Make an extra set of nametags in each of the five shapes to post at the activity stations.

SHADOW PLAY

Mixer—Find a Shadow

(Prior to the mixer, cut black construction paper into pairs of shapes, such as silhouettes of different shaped faces, or with long or short noses, or with long or short hair; hands; feet; variety of toys; bottles; crayons; hats; animals; flowers; and so on. Find a tape recording of "Me and My Shadow" or another children's shadow song.)

- As families arrive, distribute the nametags.
- Ask each family member to write his or her name on a shape nametag with a white ink pen or white marker and use masking tape to attach it to his or her clothing.
- Be sure that all members of each family have the same shape nametag so they will work together at each activity station.
- Give each participant a silhouette. Tell them that someone else in the room has a matching shadow.
- When the mixer starts, the participants try to find a silhouette that matches the one they have. When they find a match, the two participants are to introduce themselves.

*Check out the album *Dream Along with Me* by Perry Como (RCA Camden records LP12-1971).

Introduction

A shadow is a dark area produced by an object blocking light. If the object blocks light, it is opaque and makes a shadow. If the object lets light through, it is transparent and does not make a shadow. Young children have great fun playing with shadows. Beginning as tiny babies they are fascinated by the shadows they see and make. Identifying shadows can range from the very simple to more complex levels that involve abstract thinking and reasoning skills. Shadow play has a natural link to dramatic play as well as the scientific principles of light exploration.

Tell the families that they are to proceed to the station that is the same shape as their nametag. Families will move clockwise to the next station when they hear the song "Me and My Shadow" being played. The five activity stations are:

1. Shadow Portrait (face silhouette nametag)
2. Animal Hand Shadows (animal silhouette nametag)
3. What's My Job? (lunchbox silhouette nametag)
4. What's My Game? (gym shoe silhouette nametag)
5. What Am I Doing? (house silhouette nametag)

Family Meeting Activities

Station #1: Shadow Portrait

(face nametag)

Materials

Large sheets of white newsprint

Pencils

Light source, such as an overhead or film projector or
three gooseneck lamps or flashlights

Masking tape

Scissors

What to Do

1. Tape a sheet of newsprint to a wall.
2. Place the light source so it shines on the paper.
3. Ask your child to sit in front of light, casting a
   shadow that can be observed on the paper.
4. Use a pencil to draw around your child's
   silhouette that is projected on the paper.
5. Cut out the silhouette and take it home.

Station #2: Animal Hand Shadows

(animal nametag)

Materials

Light source, such as large flashlights

Instructions and examples of some hand-shadow animals (see next page)

Large bare section of wall

What to Do

(Prior to the meeting, make copies of the illustration of the hand shadows.)

1. Take one copy of the handout that illustrates a few examples of animal
   hand shadows and a flashlight.
2. Look at the examples and try making them.
3. Make animal hand shadows by shining the flashlight at a bare section
   of the wall in a dark or darkened area of the room.
4. Hold your hand or hands a few feet from the wall. When the shadow
   appears, animate the shadows by making the animal's wings flap, tails
   wag, ears wiggle, mouth open and close, and so on. For more fun, add
   your own interpretation of animal sound effects.

5. Try some of your own original animal hand shadows.
6. Notice that the closer your hands are to the light the more the light is blocked and the bigger the shadow.

SWAN

DOG: TWO EARS

BUNNY

BIRD FLAPPING WINGS

DOG, ONE EAR

Station #3: What's My Job?

(lunchbox nametag)

Materials
White sheet
Rope
Gooseneck lamp or overhead projector
Props for different occupations (e.g., hammer, drill, toilet plunger, chef's hat, large cooking pot, whisk, stirring spoon, painter's hat, paint bucket, paintbrush, paint roller and pan)
Identification cards (small cards with one of the following jobs printed on them: cooking chef, carpenter, plumber)
Boxes or large paper sacks

What to Do

Prior to the meeting, put all the props associated with one profession in a bag. Do this for all the other professions you have props for, creating as many separate bags as possible. Write the name of each occupation on an index card, and put it in the bag with the props. Put up a sheet using a rope so that participants and light source can be placed behind it.

1. Each family takes one "occupation bag."
2. Open the bag and read (silently) the occupation on the card.
3. Each family member takes a turn going behind the sheet and holding up the props from the bag to give shadow clues of the occupation each family is trying to portray. (Conceal the job props until you are behind the sheet.)
4. The rest of the group watches the shadows and tries to identify the shapes and motions that are given as clues.

Station #4: What's My Game?

(gym shoe nametag)

Materials

Large white sheet

Rope

Gooseneck lamp or overhead projector placed behind sheet

3" x 5" file cards with one of the following sports printed on them:
   baseball, soccer, tennis, badminton, football, golf, weightlifting,
   swimming, basketball (cards should be numbered 1 through 9)

Sports props: baseball bat, soccer ball, tennis racket, football, golf club,
   golf bag, small lifting weights, swim fins and snorkel mask, basketball

Nine large boxes to hold the props (Boxes should be labeled with the
   number that corresponds to the sport shadow card)

Note: Keep all props behind the sheet so they are not revealed to the participants until they take their turns creating the sport shadows.

What to Do

Prior to the meeting write different sports on index cards. Place the props for each sport in a box. Label the box and the index card with the same number. For example, label the baseball index card with number 5 and the baseball prop box with number 5.

1. Use a sheet and rope to create a curtain so that the participants and light source can be placed behind it.
2. Each family draws a card that will reveal the sport shadow that they will create behind the screen.

3. Each family takes a turn behind the screen doing the activity that they have chosen. Shadows can be made by individuals or as a group.
4. Families watching the screen will try to identify the sport.

Station #5: What Am I Doing?
(house nametag)

Materials
Large white sheet
Rope
Gooseneck lamp or overhead projector

What to Do
Prior to the meeting, use a rope to hang a sheet to create a curtain that a lamp can be placed behind.

1. Each family selects an everyday activity to act out behind the screen, such as brushing teeth, washing face, taking a bath or shower, putting on shoes, combing hair, blowing nose with handkerchief (no noise), cleaning glasses, drinking a glass of water, marching, hopping, jumping, sleeping, driving, eating, talking on the phone, and so on.
2. Each family takes a turn going behind the screen and doing three daily activities of their choice.
3. The families watching the curtain will try to identify the actions that are being portrayed.

Thank everyone for coming and invite them to share a snack of seasonal fruit and crackers after completing an evaluation form.

EVALUATION

Shadow Play

Family Meeting Evaluation

How did we do?

GREAT   POOR

Comments and Suggestions

_____

_____

_____

_____

_____

_____

_____

_____

Thank you for coming!

INVITATION

A Sound Celebration

Dear families,
You are invited to share the wonders of sound while making musical toys and creating memorable sounds.

Date _____
Time _____
Place _____

Who's Invited: The whole family

Dress: Casual

All materials as well as refreshments will be provided.

Please complete and detach the form below by _____ to reserve a space for your family.

- -

_____ Yes, we will attend "A Sound Celebration" family meeting.
_____ Sorry, we will be unable to attend the meeting.

Child's name _____
Number of adults attending _____ Number of children attending _____

If you have questions or need transportation, please call _____.

Name _____ Phone _____
Email address _____

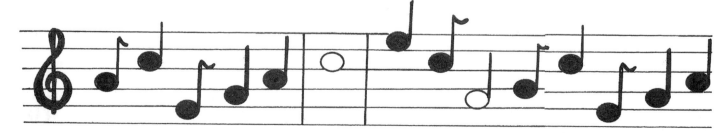

REMINDER

A Sound Celebration

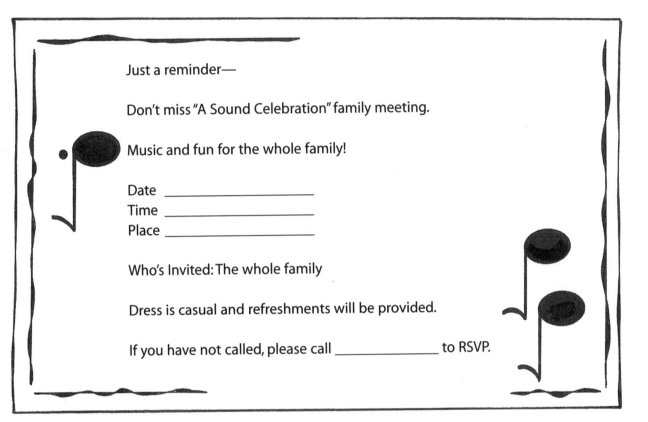

Just a reminder—

Don't miss "A Sound Celebration" family meeting.

Music and fun for the whole family!

Date _____
Time _____
Place _____

Who's Invited: The whole family

Dress is casual and refreshments will be provided.

If you have not called, please call _____ to RSVP.

Help! We need materials for this workshop. Please send or bring the following:
- empty shoeboxes
- tissue boxes
- 35 mm film canisters
- toilet paper tubes and paper towel tubes

Content Areas
Motor Skills
Music and Movement
Problem Solving
Science

Purpose
To share the wonders of sound while making musical toys and creating memorable sounds.

Related Books
Crash! Bang! Boom! by Peter Spier
The Happy Hedgehog Band by Martin Waddell

Nametags

Materials
Red, yellow, green, and orange construction paper
Markers or crayons
Scissors
Pattern for musical note nametag (see illustration)

- Use the musical note pattern (see illustration) to make nametags in four colors.
- Assign one color per family.
- Different colored nametags will be used to assign families to one of four activity stations.
- Make an extra set of nametags in each of the four colors to post at the activity stations.

Mixer

- As families arrive, distribute the musical note nametags.
- Ask each family member to write his or her name on the nametag and use masking tape to attach it to his or her clothing.
- Be sure that all members of each family have the same color nametag so they will work together at each activity station.
- Distribute one copy of " Discover Someone Who…" checklist (page 274) to each family. The families interact with each other as they try to locate people who have accomplished one of the items listed on the checklist. They should attempt to collect a different person's signature for each musical item.

Introduction

Motion is a scientific concept that is a part of everyday life. In our science program, we involve the children in activities that explore movement. Tonight we will learn how to make and play instruments that require movement or motion to make sound. We will use these sounds to play a game that we know you will not only enjoy, but will also find memorable, called "Name that Tune."

Instruct families to go to the station that has the same color as their nametag. They will have about 15 minutes to make and learn to play a musical instrument at that station. The four activity stations are:

1. Paper Roll Kazoo (red nametag)
2. Tissue Box and Shoebox Guitars (yellow nametag)
3. Sound Shakers (green nametag)
4. Soda Straw Flute (orange nametag)

Reminder: As with all family meeting activities, post the instructions at each of the stations.

Family Meeting Activities

Station #1: Paper Roll Kazoo

(red nametag)

Materials
Paper towel and toilet tissue tubes
Wax paper
Rubber bands
Scissors
Sample of a ready-to-play Kazoo

What to Do
Before the meeting, make a sample Kazoo to display.
1. Cut the wax paper into 6" (15 cm) squares.
2. Place the wax paper over one end of the tube and secure it with a rubber band.
3. To play, place your mouth over the open end of the tube and hum.
4. Practice by playing a few tunes.

Station #2: Tissue Box and Shoebox Guitars

(yellow nametag)

Materials
Tissue boxes or shoeboxes
Rubber bands (thick for low pitch and thin for high)
Sample of a ready-to-play box guitar

What to Do
Before the meeting, make a sample box guitar to display.
1. Stretch four rubber bands across a tissue box or shoebox.
2. Pluck and strum the rubber bands to play.
3. Practice a few tunes.

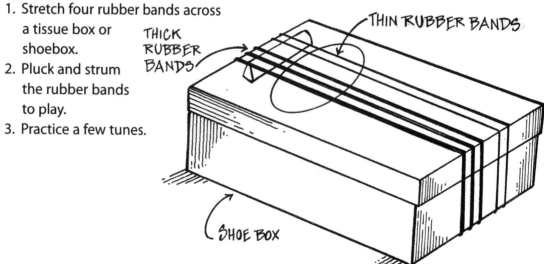

Station #3: Sound Shakers

(green nametag)

Materials

35 mm film canisters
Sand, small pebbles, pennies, and paper clips
Masking tape
Sample of a ready-to-play Sound Shaker

What to Do

Before the meeting, make a sample shaker to display.

1. Choose two empty film canisters.
2. Place a small amount of one of the ingredients in each canister and secure the lid with tape.
3. Shake the canister to play.
4. Practice a few tunes.

Station #4: Soda Straw Flute

(orange nametag)

Materials

Drinking straws
Scissors
Sample soda straw flute to display

What to Do

Before the meeting, make a sample straw flute to display.

1. Flatten one end of the straw about ¾" (2cm).
2. Use the scissors to cut two sides of the flattened portion (see illustration).
3. Play by placing the flattened end of the straw in your mouth so your lips are pressing the straw on both sides at a point beyond the cut.
4. Press your lips together slightly and blow, moving the straw back and forth while you blow. Be patient! Eventually, it will make a super sound.
5. Practice, practice, practice.

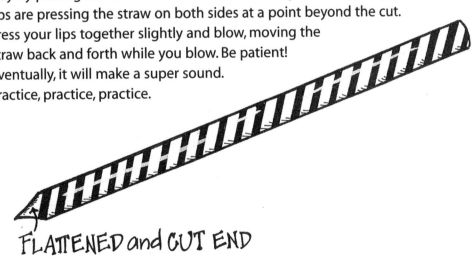

FLATTENED and CUT END

271

Group Activity

After the instruments are made, ask each of the four activity stations to select and rehearse a song to play for the entire group. As each group plays their selection, the others will try to "Name That Tune." After all the activity stations have played and the tunes have been named, bring the entire group together as an orchestra. Choose a maestro to direct the combined group in playing "Twinkle, Twinkle Little Star" or something similar that will be familiar to the children.

Note: Distribute handouts with directions on how to make all four instruments for families to take home.

Thank everyone for coming and invite them to share a snack of seasonal fruit and crackers after completing an evaluation form.

A Sound Celebration

Family Meeting Evaluation

Ask participants to circle the musical note that indicates whether the evening was a hit (whole note), just OK (1/2 note), or a flop (1/4 note).

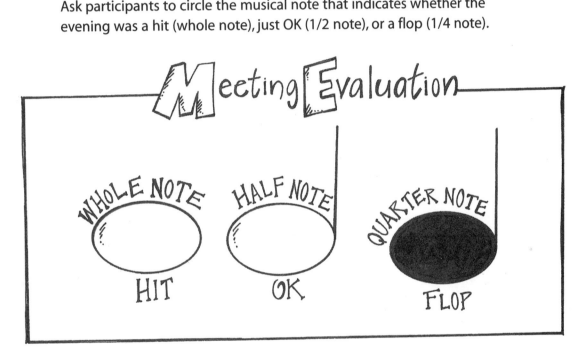

Comments and Suggestions

_____

_____

_____

_____

_____

Thank you for coming!

Discover Someone Who:

1. plays or has played a musical instrument in a school band

   _____

2. has a CD player at home

   _____

3. has a CD player in the car

   _____

4. has a name that is in the title of a song

   _____

5. knows Beethoven's first name

   _____

6. knows Chopin's first name

   _____

7. can sing tenor

   _____

8. can sing bass

   _____

9. can sing soprano

   _____

10. can sing alto

   _____

11. likes rock and roll

   _____

12. likes rap

   _____

13. likes jazz

   _____

14. likes blues

   _____

15. likes country western

   _____

16. can play "Chop Sticks" on the piano

   _____

17. knows what _crescendo_ means

   _____

18. enjoys classical music

   _____

19. has a vinyl record at home

   _____

20. can hum "Three Blind Mice"

   _____

A SOUND CELEBRATION

That's What Friends Are For

You are invited to join us for an evening of fun activities with our friends!

Join us as we explore the world of friendship as we share, care, and practice good manners.

We believe social development and awareness is a must for young learners, so we have developed activities encouraging positive social growth while focusing on friendship. We hope you can join us for the evening.

Date _____

Time _____

Place _____

Who's Invited: The whole family

Please dress casually.

Refreshments will be served.

Please complete and detach the form below by _____ to reserve a space for your family.

_____ Yes, we will attend the "That's What Friends Are For" family meeting.
_____ Sorry, we are unable to attend the meeting.

Child's name _____

Number of adults attending _____ Number of children attending _____

Need transportation? Yes___ No ___

If you have questions or need transportation, please call _____.

Name _____ Phone _____

Email address _____

That's What Friends Are For

Just a reminder about the "That's What Friends Are For" family meeting.

Explore the world of friendship as we share, care, and practice good manners.

Date _____
Time _____
Place _____

Who's Invited: The whole family

Please dress casually.

If you have any questions, please call us at _____. If you didn't have a chance to respond, there's still time.

Simply call _____ to reserve a spot as soon as possible.

Snacks will be provided.

Thank you!

Content Areas

Art
Literacy
Math
Problem Solving
Social Development

Purpose

To develop children's decision-making and problem-solving skills, and to help them learn how to solve conflicts in positive ways and choose to be kind and responsible.

Nametags

Materials

Red, yellow, green, and pink construction paper
Scissors
Strawberry pattern (see below)
Markers

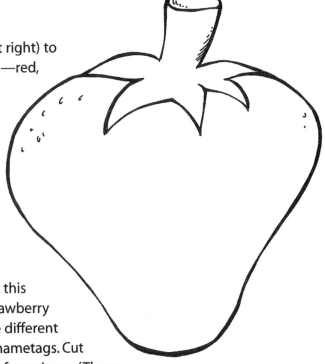

- Use the strawberry pattern (at right) to make nametags in four colors—red, pink, yellow, and green.
- Assign one color per family.
- Different-colored nametags will be used to assign families to one of four activity stations.
- Make an extra set of nametags in each of the four colors to post at the activity stations.
- Enlarge the nametag and use this larger strawberry to make strawberry puzzles in four colors that are different from the colors used for the nametags. Cut these larger strawberries into four pieces. (These strawberry puzzles will be used for the mixer activity.)

Mixer

- As families arrive, distribute the strawberry nametags.
- Ask each family member to write his or her name on the strawberry and use masking tape to attach it to his or her clothing.
- Be sure to keep the number of people at each activity station as equal as possible, and keep family members at the same station. Inform the families that they will begin at the station with the strawberry that is the same color as their nametag.
- Assemble the group in a meeting area. Read *The Little Mouse, The Red Ripe Strawberry, and The Big Hungry Bear* by Don and Audrey Wood.
- Give each participant one piece of the large strawberry puzzles (see nametag directions).
- Explain that each participant will need to find the three other people who have the pieces that fit with their strawberry piece.
- Once they have found all the pieces to their strawberry, everyone should introduce himself or herself by saying their name and one nice thing someone has done for them recently.

Introduction

This family meeting focuses on several aspects of friendship, including caring and sharing. Activities at the stations stress the importance of sharing and caring (including bookmaking, problem solving, and socialization skills). Remember how important it is for adults to set good examples in situations that require decision making and problem solving. It is equally important to present situations that allow children to make their own decisions. Remember to praise them when they act responsibly and kindly.

Ask families to go to the station with the colored strawberry that matches their nametag. Ask them to listen for a signal to let them know they have two to three minutes before rotating. When they hear the next signal, they should move clockwise to the next activity station. Signals to consider using are playing music, flickering the lights on and off, or playing a tambourine or triangle. The four activity stations are:

1. One for You…One for Me (red strawberry nametag)
2. I Can Share, Too! (pink strawberry nametag)
3. Manners, Please (green strawberry nametag)
4. Same, But Different! (yellow strawberry nametag)

Family Meeting Activities

Station #1: One for You...One for Me

(red strawberry nametag)

The concept of sharing equally can be hard for young children to understand. At this station, children will use their problem-solving skills to determine how to divide items equally so everyone gets the same number.

Materials
Bear, mouse, and child patterns—1 set for each child (see next page)
Buttons, counters, or other small items (approximately 12 per child)

What to Do
Before the meeting, cut out bear, mouse, and child patterns so there will be enough for each child who is coming to the meeting. If desired, laminate the patterns.

1. Give your child a bear, a mouse, and a child pattern, as well as 12 buttons, which represent cookies.
2. Tell your child these are three friends who have been playing together. They are hungry and want to share some "cookies."
3. Ask your child to divide the cookies (buttons) so each of the friends will have the same number.
4. Once your child has given the cookies to each character, count the cookies together to see if they all have the same number. If not, encourage your child to try another way of dividing the cookies.
5. If your child has made a few attempts and still has an unequal number of cookies for the friends, offer suggestions so your child does not become frustrated.
6. After the cookies have been divided equally, pretend one of the friends has to go home. Divide the cookies between two friends.
7. Talk about how the problem was solved. Praise and encourage your child frequently!

THAT'S WHAT FRIENDS ARE FOR

Station #2: I Can Share, Too!

(pink nametag)

Reinforce the importance of sharing while creating pages for a book that shows ways to share things with friends.

Materials
18" x 12" white construction paper
Crayons or markers

What to Do
1. As a group, talk about times you shared something with a friend. Tell how you felt and how the person you shared with felt.
2. After everyone has had a chance to share, ask your child to draw a picture of a time he or she shared something with a friend.
3. Ask your child to tell you about the picture. As the child dictates, write what the child says below the picture (or above, or wherever there might be room!).
4. Put your child's name on his or her picture.
5. Stack the pictures in a designated area so they can be assembled into a book.

Station #3: Manners, Please

(green nametag)

Politeness and the use of good manners show that children are developing good social skills. Role play is a good way to encourage the use of good manners.

Materials
Tables
Chairs
Plates, cups, napkins, utensils
Pretend food
Notepads and pencils
Cashier register
Aprons
Timer
Note: Restaurant materials may vary depending on what is available at your center or school.

What to Do

Before the meeting, decorate the activity station to represent a restaurant.

1. As a group, work together to decide which roles each person will play (customer, cashiers, waiter/waitress).
2. Act out the roles for five minutes.
2. Rotate roles every five minutes.
3. Demonstrate good manners, including saying, "Please," "Thank you," and "Excuse me."
4. When it's time to move to another station, return all materials to their original location so the station is ready for the next group.

Station #4: Same, But Different!

(yellow nametag)

Part of being a good friend includes understanding and accepting differences. Participants team up with others at the station to see how they are alike and how they are different.

Materials

Paper
Crayons

What to Do

1. Find a partner. It can be someone from your family or someone from another family at this station.
2. One set of partners stands in front of the rest of the group.
3. The group describes two ways the partners are the same and two ways they are different.
4. Before rejoining the group, each partner says, "I like you because..." (completing the sentence with a compliment).
5. After everyone has had a turn, each person draws a picture of him- or herself with their partner.

Distribute evaluation forms and invite the group for a snack of heart-shaped sugar cookies and juice.

EVALUATION

That's What Friends Are For

Family Meeting Evaluation

Please color in the heart that shows how you felt about tonight's meeting. Your comments are important to us. Thank you!

I loved the meeting.   The meeting was okay.   I'm brokenhearted—I didn't care for the meeting.

Comments and Suggestions

_____

_____

_____

_____

_____

_____

Thank you for coming!

INVITATION

Water Works: Fun With Water

Children are intrigued by water. Come to this family meeting to learn how this natural fascination with a basic ingredient of life makes learning about water fun.

Who's Invited: The whole family

Dress: Casual

Refreshments will be served.

Please complete and detach the form below by _____ to reserve a space for your family.

PLACE:

DATE:

TIME:

OBSERVING

PREDICTING

COMPARING

MEASURING

_____ Yes, we will attend the "Water Works" family meeting.
_____ Sorry, we are unable to attend the meeting.

Child's name _____
Number of adults attending _____
Number of children attending _____

If you have any questions or need transportation, please call _____

Name _____
Phone _____
Email address _____

REMINDER

Water Works: Fun With Water

Don't forget the "Water Works:
Fun With Water" Family Meeting!

It promises to be a wet and wild time for all.

Who: Your family

What: A family meeting

Date _____
Time _____
Place _____

Why: To discover the secrets of water
Dress: Casual

Refreshments will be served.

Call _____ if you haven't made your reservation.

Content Areas

Math
Motor Skills
Problem Solving
Science

Purpose

To present activities that enable families to discover the secrets of water.

Related Books

A Cold Drink of Water by Barbara Kerley
A Drop of Water by Walter Wick
Precious Water, A Book of Thanks by Brigitte Weninger and Anne Moller

Nametags

Materials

Construction paper (red, yellow, white, blue, and green)
Scissors
Markers
Water drop pattern (see below)

- Use the water drop pattern (at right) to cut out nametags in five colors.
- Assign one color per family.
- Different colored nametags will be used to assign families to one of five activity stations.
- Make an extra set of nametags in each of the five colors to post at the activity stations.

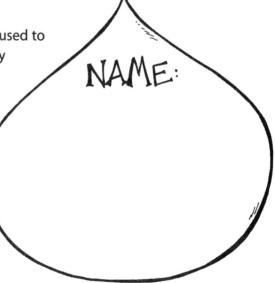

Mixer—Beach Ball Toss

- As families arrive, distribute the water drop nametags.
- Ask each family member to write his or her name on the water drop and use masking tape to attach it to his or her clothing.
- Be sure all members of each family have the same color nametag so they will work together at each activity station.
- Form a large circle with all the participants of the family meeting.
- Hold a beach ball and state your name and one activity you enjoy doing that involves water, such as swimming, sailing, washing the car, or showering.
- Toss the beach ball to another person who catches the ball and repeats the process.
- Continue until all participants have an opportunity to share.

Introduction

The activities in this family meeting explore water's scientific wonders. Children will enjoy repeating these activities at home. Activities reinforce the scientific processes of observation, classification, measurement, prediction, inference, and developing pre-science communication skills.

Ask families to move to the activity station that has the same color as their water drop nametag. They will remain at that center until they hear the timer bell. At the signal, families move clockwise as they rotate to the next station. The five activity stations are:

1. Hold Tight, Mr. Lincoln (red water drop nametag)
2. Water Magnifiers (yellow water drop nametag)
3. Bubbles, Bubbles, Bubbles (white water drop nametag)
4. Water Drop Racers (blue water drop nametag)
5. Musical Cups (green water drop nametag)

WATER WORKS: FUN WITH WATER

Family Meeting Activities

Station #1: Hold Tight, Mr. Lincoln

(red nametag)

Water has a stronger surface tension than most liquids. This activity is an experiment to show how strong water is.

Materials
Pipettes or eyedroppers
Pennies
Clear plastic cup (1 oz.)
Water
Paper towels
Plastic containers or small dishpan to hold water
Paper
Pencils

What to Do
1. Each family takes a penny, a pipette, paper towel, and a small sheet of paper and a pencil to record estimates and findings.
2. Estimate or predict (guess) how many drops of water will fit on your penny before it spills over the side of the coin. Record the guesses.
3. Place the penny on the paper towel.
4. Fill the pipette or eyedropper with water. Carefully drip water drops on the penny and count aloud as the drops fall on the penny. When the water falls over the side of the penny, record that number on the tally sheet. Compare the number of drops to your estimate.
5. Try it again using the other side of the penny.
6. Extend this activity by filling a 1 oz. cup to the brim with water. Each participant takes a turn carefully dropping a penny into the cup.
7. As the pennies are dropped into the cup, a dome of water will appear just as it did with the penny. Observe how high the dome can go before it overflows.

Note: Many variables come into play here, including size of the water drops, height of pipette from the coin, and the patience of the participant. It is best to do both water tension activities with the children before the meeting so they can teach their parents. It's always a winner!

For adult information only: Water molecules attract each other. They hug each other and form a surface that is not easily penetrated. A water molecule in the center of the cup is pulled equally in all directions. Since there are no water molecules above the surface, the molecules at the surface are pulled more closely together, allowing them to create a dome which you will observe as you carefully drop the water on the face of the coin.

Station #2: Water Magnifiers
(yellow nametag)

One of the first tools of science is a magnifier for making regular size things look larger. Water is a natural magnifier—a single drop of water can magnify the underlying surface.

Materials
Wax paper cut into 4" x 4" squares
Eyedroppers or pipettes
Newspaper cut into 4" x 4" squares
Water in a bowl
Example of a larger magnifier

What to Do
Before the meeting, make a large magnifier from a large paper fried chicken bucket to show as a model (see next page).
1. Each family takes one piece of wax paper, one eyedropper or pipette, and one piece of newspaper.
2. Use the eyedropper or pipette to drop one drop of water on the wax paper.
3. Observe how easily the water drop moves on the paper and is not absorbed.
4. Slide a piece of newspaper under the wax paper. Look through the drop of water at the print. What has happened to the size of the print?
5. Predict what will happen if a larger or smaller drop of water is placed over it.
6. Look at the model magnifier made from a fried chicken bucket. To make this at home, you will need a large fried chicken bucket with the top and bottom removed. Cut a piece of clear plastic wrap about 1" larger than the top of the bucket. Place the wrap loosely over the top and secure it with a rubber band. Pour $\frac{1}{3}$ cup of water onto the plastic wrap. The weight of the water will make the wrap sag.
7. Place the bucket over a coin, leaf, or any other object and observe and compare the magnification of objects with this magnifier as compared with the magnifier created in the first three steps of this activity.

NEWSPAPER

WAX PAPER

CLEAR PLASTIC WRAP (1" larger than opening)

CUT BOTH ENDS OFF

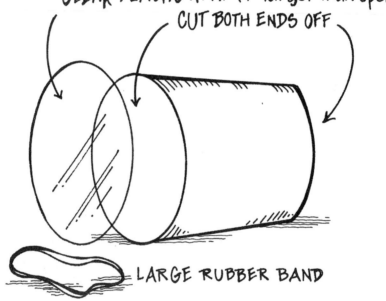

LARGE RUBBER BAND

WATER

Station #3: Bubbles, Bubbles, Bubbles
(white water drop nametag)

Explore color, shape, and solutions while having a great time.

Materials
Containers to hold bubble solution
Plastic straws, string, pipe cleaners, plastic rings from soda six-packs, paper cups with bottoms removed, or plastic mesh strawberry baskets
4 large cookie baking sheets
Paper towels

Recipe for Bubble Mixture (double or triple depending on group size)
$\frac{1}{3}$ cup of liquid soap
1 cup water
1 teaspoon sugar

What to Do
Before the meeting, prepare the bubble solution.
1. Pour bubble solution onto the four cookie sheets to a depth of $\frac{1}{3}$".
2. Make bubble-making instruments by shaping pipe cleaners or removing the bottoms of paper cups.
3. Make a rectangular bubble blower using two drinking straws and string by looping the string through the two straws and tying it (see illustration).
4. Use six-pack containers and mesh baskets to create multiple bubble makers.
5. Blow away!

STRING   STRAWS

For adult information only: Water molecules are attracted to each other, and when mixed with a soap solution, they get very close (like skin). Regardless of the shape of the bubble-making instrument, the bubbles will be round as the solution tries to join together as the air in the bubble is pushing out. The round shape allows the solution to get as close together as possible.

Station #4: Water Drop Racers

(blue water drop nametag)

This activity is a way to investigate how water drops form and move on different surfaces, and to observe two properties of water—adhesion and cohesion. Cohesion is the ability of substances to stick together. Put a drop of water on the surface of the ramp. Keep adding drops to this first drop. Observe the drop as it becomes larger and larger until gravity pulls it down the ramp. Adhesion is the ability to stick to a different substance. Drop water onto different surfaces and see whether the type of surface affects the formation and movement of the drops.

Materials

Eyedroppers or pipettes
Containers of water
Variety of surface materials, such as wax paper, aluminum foil, newsprint, and sandpaper to cover ramps
4 cookie sheets—one for each surface material (more if the group size is larger than four families)
Blocks
Paper towels

What to Do

Before the meeting, prepare the ramps. Label each one with the name of the attached surface.

1. Each family uses one of the cookie sheets.
2. Tip cookie sheets at a slight angle. Rest one end on a block or a book. All ramps should be at the same angle.
3. Use an eyedropper or pipette to put a line of water drops on the surface.
4. Continue adding droplets until the water begins to run down the cookie sheet. How many drops does it take before it runs?
5. Trade cookie sheets, to try all the surfaces. Do the water drops run faster or slower? Which ones do you think have the fastest surfaces for the Water Drop Racers?

Station #5: Musical Cups

(green nametag)

Vibrations cause sounds. Water and friction are used in this activity to create an instrument that makes weird sounds.

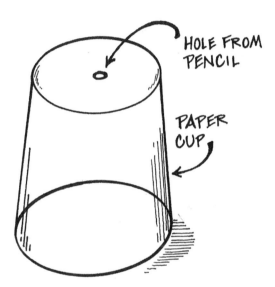

Materials
Paper cups of various sizes
Paper clips
String
Small containers of water
Scissors
Pencils

What to Do
1. Use a pencil to punch a hole in the bottom of the paper cup.
2. Cut a 12"-15" (30-45 cm) length of string. Insert the string into the hole.
3. Tie a paper clip inside the cup and pull into place.
4. Soak the string with water. It must be very wet.
5. Place two fingers around the string and hold firmly as your fingers slide downward. Listen for the "herd of elephants."

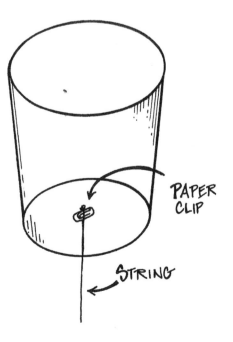

Thank everyone for coming and invite them to share a snack of seasonal fruit and crackers after completing an evaluation form.

EVALUATION

Water Works: Fun With Water

Family Meeting Evaluation

We would like to know what you thought about the "Water Works" family meeting. Please circle the picture that best describes your feelings. We appreciate your feedback, so feel free to make comments. Thank you.

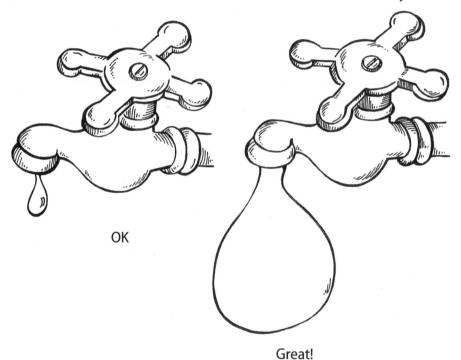

OK

Great!

Comments and Suggestions

_____

_____

_____

_____

Thank you for coming!

INVITATION

The World Is a Rainbow

The  is a

Come join us for fun activities that develop an appreciation and awareness of the unique attributes of each family.

You're Invited!

Date _____
Time _____
Place _____

Who's Invited: The whole family

Dress: Casual

Refreshments will be served.

Please complete and detach the form below by _____ to reserve a space for your family.

- -

_____ Yes, we will attend "The World Is a Rainbow" family meeting.
_____ Sorry, we are unable to attend the meeting.

Child's name _____
Number of adults attending _____ Number of children attending _____

If you have any questions or need transportation, please call _____.

Name _____ Phone _____
Email address _____

© Gryphon House, Inc. 800.638.0928 www.gryphonhouse.com

The World Is a Rainbow

Just a note to remind you of "The World Is a Rainbow " family meeting.

Date _____

Time _____

Place _____

At this family meeting we will do hands-on activities that support positive attitudes toward all people around the world.

Dress: Casual

Who's Invited? The whole family

Goodies provided for everyone!

Content Area
Multicultural Awareness

Purpose
To increase awareness of the importance of multicultural education through developmentally appropriate activities that support positive attitudes toward diversity.

Related Books
All Kinds of Children by Norma Simon
Extraordinary Friends by Fred Rogers
Families by Ann Morris

Nametags

Materials
Red, yellow, blue, and orange construction paper
Scissors
Globe pattern (see below)
Markers

- Use the globe pattern (see below) to make nametags in four colors.
- Assign one color per family.
- Different colored nametags will be used to assign families to one of four activity stations.
- Make an extra set of nametags in each of the four colors to post at the activity stations.

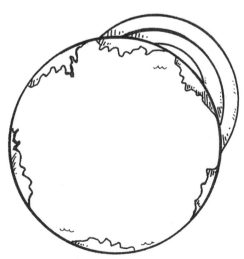

Mixer—Where's Your Family From?

- As families arrive, distribute the globe nametags.
- Ask each family member to write his or her name on the globe and use masking tape to attach it to his or her clothing.
- Be sure all members of each family have the same color nametag so they will work together at each activity station.
- Ask everyone to stand in a circle. Members of each family should stand together.
- Toss a globe ball (or any ball) to one participant.
- The family member holding the globe gives the family name, introduces family members present, and says the name of the country (or countries) of the family's origin.
- Toss the globe to another family and repeat this procedure until all families have been introduced.
- If possible, ask each family to put a colored push-pin on a world map that is hanging on the wall.

Introduction

Between the ages of two and five, children form self-identities and build social interaction skills. At the same time, they become aware of and are curious about gender, race, ethnicity, and disabilities. Gradually, young children figure out how they are different from other people and how they feel about those differences. Learning about people, their similarities and their differences, is fundamental to addressing social and global issues. The activities in this family meeting will help families understand and appreciate our differences and our similarities.

Tell families to go to the activity station that matches the color of their nametag. When they hear or see a signal (a bell ringing, a whistle blowing, or the lights flickering off and on), it means that it is time to move clockwise to the next activity station. The four activity stations are:

1. I'm Thumb-Body Special (yellow globe)
2. All Colors Are Beautiful (red globe)
3. Hands Around the World (orange globe)
4. We Are Special (blue globe)

Family Meeting Activities

Station #1: I'm Thumb-Body Special

(yellow nametag)

Develops awareness of individual differences.

Materials
Inkpads
Hand wipes
Magnifying glasses
3" x 5" index cards
3' x 2' poster board
Tape or glue

What to Do
1. Everyone makes a thumbprint on seperate index cards.
2. Write your name on your card. (Help those who need it.)
3. Examine the prints with a magnifying glass.
4. Attach your thumbprint card to the 3' x 2' poster board using tape or glue.
5. After all cards have been attached, re-examine all of the thumbprints closely using a magnifying glass.
6. Talk about what you see.

Note: While we are alike in many ways, one way we differ is that the line patterns on our fingers are different. These patterns are called fingerprints, and no two are alike. They help make each of us unique and special.

Station #2: All Colors Are Beautiful

(red nametag)

Develops and enhances an appreciation of our skin color.

Materials
Group color photo of all the children and staff members
Magnifying glasses or hand lens

What to Do
1. As a group, talk about the colors in the world and in the room. Talk about how people come in all colors too, with many different colors and shades of skin.
2. Look at the group photo of the children and staff. What skin colors do you see in this picture?

3. Each family takes a magnifying glass or hand lens. Take a close look at your skin.

4. Each participant puts his or her arm in a circle. Compare skin colors.

For adult information only: Give a brief overview of melanin and how it helps to block dangerous rays from the sun. We all have it. The more melanin in the skin, the darker the skin's color. When the sun shines on the skin, melanin absorbs as many rays as possible. It helps to prevent our skin from burning.

Station #3: Hands Around the World

(orange globe nametag)

Develops an awareness of individual differences.

Materials
Multi-colored construction paper
Scissors
Masking tape
Markers
Globe or world map

What to Do
1. Trace and cut out your handprint on the paper that most closely resembles your skin color. (Help those who need it.)
2. Compare your hand size and color with other participants' hand size and color.
3. Tape the handprints together and wrap them around the globe or across the world map.

Station #4: We Are Special

(blue nametag)

Develops an appreciation and an awareness of the unique attributes of each family.

Materials
Paper
Pencils or markers

What to Do
1. Brainstorm and list the positive attributes that make your family special.
2. Share your list with the other participants.
3. As a group, sing the following to the tune of "Frere Jacques."

We are special. (point to selves)
We are special.
If you look (point to others)
You will see.
We are very special,
We are very special.
That is us. (point to selves)
That is us.

EVALUATION

The World Is a Rainbow

Family Meeting Evaluation

Color the number of lines in the rainbow.

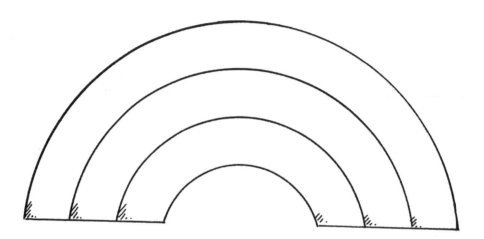

One line colored = average meeting
Two lines colored = a better than average meeting
Three lines colored = an excellent meeting

Comments and Suggestions

_____

_____

_____

_____

_____

_____

_____

Thanks for coming!

BOOK LIST

Bananas About Books
Here Comes Mother Goose by
   Iona Opie
My Very First Mother Goose by
   Iona Opie

Bright Ideas
A Chair for My Mother by Vera B.
   Williams
Joseph Had a Little Overcoat by
   Simms Taback
Somewhere Today by Shelley Moore
   Thomas

Cool Kids Cooking
Pretend Soup and Other Real Recipes
   by Mollie Katzen and Ann
   Henderson

**Discovering Our Unique
Qualities**
The Carrot Seed by Ruth Krauss
The Little House by Virginia Lee
   Burton
Mike Mulligan and His Steam Shovel
   by Virginia Lee Burton
Stand Tall, Molly Lou Melon by Patty
   Lovell
The Story of Ferdinand by Munro Leaf

Exploring Our Community
Career Day by Anne Rockwell
Firefighters A to Z by Chris L.
   Demarest
Night Shift Daddy by Eileen Spinelli

Exploring Our Senses
Mabela the Clever by Margaret Read
   MacDonald
My Five Senses by Aliki

Family Bookworms
(see page 123)

Get Ready, Get Set, Move!
From Head to Toe by Eric Carle
Good Thing You're Not an Octopus by
   Julie Markes
Here Are My Hands by Bill Martin, Jr.
   and John Archambault

Great Graphing Safari
Castles, Caves, and Honeycombs by
   Linda Ashman (home preference)
Chicka Chicka Boom Boom by Bill
   Martin, Jr. and John Archambault
   (naming)
The Colors of Us by Karen Katz
   (personal physical qualities)
Houses and Homes by Ann Morris
   (home and food preferences)
I Love My Hair by Natasha Anastasia
   Tarpley (personal physical
   qualities)
We All Sing with the Same Voice by J.
   Philip Miller and Sheppard M.
   Greene (personal physical abilities)

Magical Art Mixtures
Cool Ali by Nancy Poydar
Mouse Painting by Ellen Stoll Walsh

Meaningful Math
Five Creatures by Emily Jenkins
Millions of Cats by Wanda Gag
Eating Fractions by Bruce McMillan

More Than Crayons and Brushes
Harold and the Purple Crayon by
   Crockett Johnson

Move Out to Check it Out
Fall Is Not Easy by Marty Kelley
In the Small, Small Pond by Denise
   Fleming
In the Tall, Tall Grass by Denise Fleming
Ugh! A Bug by Mary Bono
*Where Does the Butterfly Go When It
   Rains?* by May Garelick

Number Fun Family Night
Let's Count by Tana Hoban
Low Song by Eve Merriam
One, Two, Skip a Few by
   Roberta Arenson

Raisin' Your Nutritional IQ
I Eat Fruit by Hannah Tofts
I Eat Vegetables by Hannah Tofts
I Will Never Not Ever Eat a Tomato by
   Lauren Child

Scientific Art
*Brown Bear, Brown Bear, What Do You
   See?* by Bill Martin, Jr.
Freight Train by Donald Crews
Go Away, Big Green Monster! by
   Ed Emberly
Little Blue and Little Yellow by
   Leo Lionni

Shadow Play
Guess Whose Shadow? by Stephen R.
   Swinburne
*Mother, Mother I Feel Sick, Send for
   the Doctor, Quick Quick Quick* by
   Remy Charlip
My Shadow by Robert Louis Stevenson

A Sound Celebration
Crash! Bang! Boom! by Peter Spier
The Happy Hedgehog Band by Martin
   Waddell

Water Works
A Cold Drink of Water by Barbara Kerley
A Drop of Water by Walter Wick
Precious Water, A Book of Thanks by
   Brigitte Weninger and Anne Moller

The World Is a Rainbow
All Kinds of Children by Norma Simon
Extraordinary Friends by Fred Rogers
Families by Ann Morris

BOOK LIST

INDEX

305

BOOK INDEX

Early Learning Environments That Work

Rebecca Isbell and Betty Exelby

The classroom environment is a vital part of a child's learning experience. *Early Learning Environments That Work* explores how you can work with furniture, color, materials, storage, lighting, and more to encourage learning through classroom arrangement. Each chapter gives you detailed illustrations and photographs to help you set up or arrange what you already have in the classroom. 192 pages. 2001.
ISBN 0-87659-256-6 / Gryphon House 14387 / PB

Early Childhood Workshops That Work!

The Essential Guide to Successful Workshops and Training
Nancy P. Alexander

This comprehensive guide illustrates how to design, organize, conduct, and evaluate effective workshop and training seminars. It also includes sections on troubleshooting and designing learning materials. *Early Childhood Workshops That Work!* shows you how to make your training effective, interactive, and rewarding! 192 pages. 2000.
ISBN 0-87659-215-9 / Gryphon House 13876 / PB

Available at your favorite bookstore, school supply store, or order from Gryphon House at 800.638.0928 or www.gryphonhouse.com.

The Practical Guide to Quality Child Care

Pam Schiller and Patricia Carter Dyke

This uniquely comprehensive manual is a clear, easy-to-read handbook that provides specific guidelines for virtually every aspect of early childhood administration. Contents include sample forms, procedures for program development, schedules, applications, and evaluations. An invaluable tool for every child care facility manager. 192 pages. 2001.
ISBN 0-87659-262-0 / Gryphon House 17356 / PB

Solutions for Early Childhood Directors

Real Answers to Everyday Issues
Kathy Lee

Handling discipline, hiring and training staff, dealing with parents, handling special-needs children, and creating partnerships in the community… these are just a few issues that early childhood program directors tackle every day. Written by an experienced director of early childhood programs, this book will serve any director as mentor, best friend, and can't-do-without-it guide to this rich and complex profession. 224 pages.
ISBN 0-87659-229-9 / Gryphon House 17564 / PB

Available at your favorite bookstore, school supply store, or order from Gryphon House at 800.638.0928 or www.gryphonhouse.com.

Mudpies to Magnets

A Preschool Science Curriculum

Robert A. Williams, Robert E. Rockwell, and Elizabeth A. Sherwood

224 hands-on science experiments and ideas, with step-by-step instructions, to delight and amaze children as they experience nature, the human body, electricity, floating and sinking, and more. 157 pages. 1987.

ISBN 0-87659-112-8 / Gryphon House 10005 / PB

More Mudpies to Magnets

Science for Young Children

Elizabeth A. Sherwood, Robert A. Williams, and Robert E. Rockwell

Develop the natural scientist in every child with 260 hands-on science activities and ideas. Build science skills such as classification, measurement, time and space concepts, prediction, inference, and numbers. 205 pages. 1990.

ISBN 0-87659-150-0 / Gryphon House 10015 / PB

Available at your favorite bookstore, school supply store, or order from Gryphon House at 800.638.0928 or www.gryphonhouse.com.

Everybody Has a Body

Science from Head to Toe

Robert E. Rockwell, Robert A. Williams, and Elizabeth A. Sherwood

Children discover the magic of science as they learn about their bodies. 268 easy-to-do activities promote observation, inference, and prediction skills. 250 pages. 1992.
ISBN 0-87659-158-6 / Gryphon House 10027 / PB

Linking Language

Simple Language and Literacy Activities Throughout the Curriculum

Robert Rockwell, Debra Hoge, and Bill Searcy

Filled with practical, everyday activities to build language development and early literacy into your daily schedule. Use circle time, snack time, dramatic play, or any time throughout the day to develop children's language skills. Each cross-curricular activity includes ways to enhance children's vocabularies, questions to help the teacher evaluate children's progress, an annotated list of books that relate to the activity, and age-appropriate suggestions for writing experiences. 227 pages. 1999.
ISBN 0-87659-202-7 / Gryphon House 17561 / PB

Available at your favorite bookstore, school supply store, or order from Gryphon House at
800.638.0928 or www.gryphonhouse.com.

319